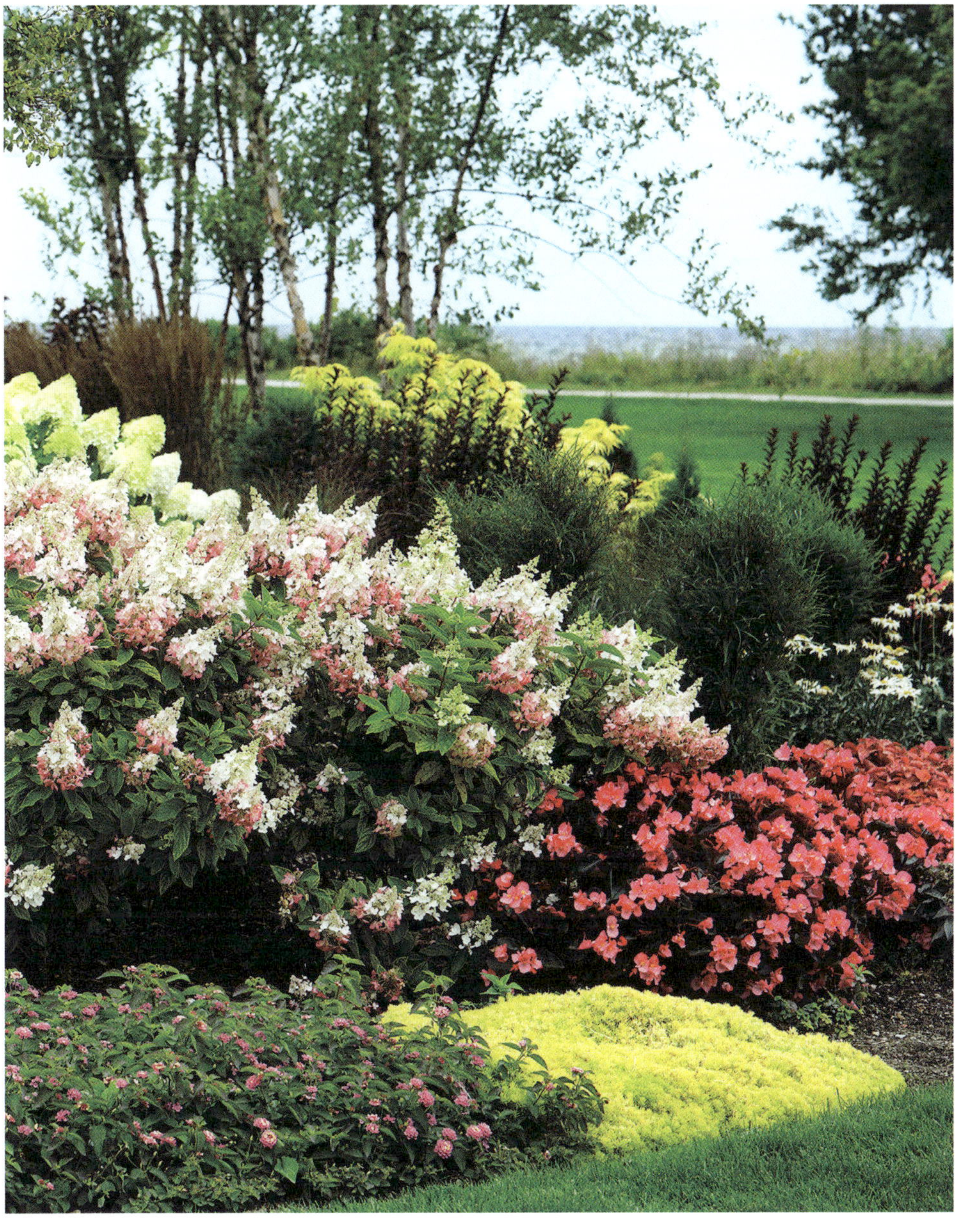

Birds&Blooms

Gardening Secrets

Sunflowers provide nectar for butterflies, such as monarchs, and seeds for birds, page 36

Table of Contents

5 **INTRODUCTION**

6 **CHAPTER 1**
Spring

70 **CHAPTER 2**
Summer

136 **CHAPTER 3**
Fall

192 **CHAPTER 4**
Winter

226 **CHAPTER 5**
Indoor Gardening

FRONT COVER PHOTOS
Clockwise from top: Jane Work; Kate Wieser, Claudia Totir, Annie Otzen/ Getty Images (3)

TITLE PAGE PHOTO
Courtesy of Proven Winners - www.provenwinners.com

BACK COVER PHOTO
Right: John Gill

CHIEF CONTENT OFFICER
Jason Buhrmester

CONTENT DIRECTOR
Kirsten Schrader

CREATIVE DIRECTOR
Raeann Thompson

ASSOCIATE CREATIVE DIRECTOR
Kristen Stecklein

EDITORS Srinwanti Das, Megan White

MANAGER, PRODUCTION DESIGN
Satyandra Raghav

SENIOR PRINT PUBLICATION DESIGNER Sanjeev Dhiman

PRINT PUBLICATION DESIGNER
Mukesh Kumar

PRINT PRODUCTION ARTIST
Akash Christopher

DEPUTY EDITOR, COPY DESK
Ann M. Walter

SENIOR COPY EDITORS
Elizabeth Pollock Bruch, Suchismita Ukil

ASSOCIATE COPY EDITOR
Rachana Rana

A *Birds & Blooms* Book

ISBNs
979-8-88977-123-4 (Hardcover)
979-8-88977-173-9 (Paperback)

Component Number 118500130H

For more *Birds & Blooms* products and information, visit our website: *www.birdsandblooms.com*.

Hardcover printed in China
10 9 8 7 6 5 4 3 2 1

Paperback printed in China
10 9 8 7 6 5 4 3 2 1

Text, photography and illustrations for *Gardening Secrets* are based on articles previously published in *Birds & Blooms* magazine (*www.birdsandblooms.com*).

Female ruby-throated hummingbird at salvia, *page 75*

Violas, *page 219*

Seasonal Delight!

Celebrate gardening in every season—because there's always something to dig into! From the first cheerful blooms of spring to summer's veggie bonanza, and from the golden leaves of fall to the annual winter pruning, there's magic waiting in your yard year-round. So grab your gloves, roll up your sleeves and let the good times grow—because every season is garden season! And with *Gardening Secrets* by your side, you're set up for success.

—THE EDITORS OF
BIRDS & BLOOMS MAGAZINE

CHAPTER 1

Spring

From bird-loving blooms to genius garden hacks for pollinators, composting magic and water-saving tricks—unlock the secrets to a dreamy spring backyard oasis.

Garden Myths Debunked!

A lot of fantastic gardening advice has been passed down through the generations, but some erroneous recommendations have trickled down as well. Here are 10 myths that can be officially laid to rest.

By Luke Miller

Myth: Compost Smells Awful.

FACT: If your compost pile has anything but a pleasant earthy smell, it's not being properly worked. Anaerobic composting means there might be a lack of oxygen in the pile. It will break down—slowly—but will have a swampy smell. Turn the pile regularly to introduce oxygen and help mitigate any odor. Add dry leaves and a few shovels full of soil to keep materials from turning slimy.

Myth: To Ripen Green Tomatoes, Set Them on a Sunny Windowsill.

FACT: Sunlight is not needed. For slow ripening, put tomatoes in a cool basement and wrap them individually in newspaper to contain the ethylene gas given off by the fruit that hastens ripening. Store ripe and unripe fruits together for faster results.

Fresh as a Daisy
Turn compost piles regularly to introduce enough oxygen and prevent a strong smell.

FROM LEFT: FOCUS35; ULIU/GETTY IMAGES

Myth: You Need to Water Plants Daily.

FACT: Container plants may need a dousing daily, but those in landscapes do not. It's better to water once or twice a week and to irrigate deeply. Shallow watering encourages roots to stay near the surface. Instead, you want roots to grow deep so plants are self-sufficient during dry periods. Obviously, cactuses and succulents need less water. Check the soil moisture before getting the hose out.

Myth: You Should Paint Tree Wounds After Pruning.

FACT: This is an old practice of tree care that has fallen out of favor. In most cases, painting a blemish doesn't serve a purpose and may actually negatively affect the sealing of the wound. However, there are exceptions: If you are pruning a tree that could be threatened by the disease-carrying beetles attracted to a fresh wound, tree-wound paint can help. Consider it for the types of oaks that are susceptible to oak wilt in particular.

Myth: You Can't Grow Anything Near a Black Walnut Tree.

FACT: While black walnut trees do release an allelopathic chemical called juglone, which can inhibit the growth of some plants, many others are able to grow beneath and near them. Zinnia, daylily, phlox, shasta daisy, begonia, Japanese maple, forsythia and purple coneflower all are capable of thriving nearby. Your local cooperative extension or master gardener program will have a complete list for your region.

Black walnut

Myth: For the Best Garden Soil, Be Sure to Cultivate Regularly.

FACT: Some cultivation is helpful with heavy or compacted soils but too much can turn the topsoil into a powdery dust that repels water and is not conducive to root growth. Also, frequent cultivation exposes more of the soil to the sun, which can dry it out and cut down the amount of beneficial microbes.

Myth: Newspaper and Cardboard Are Great Weed Barriers.

FACT: In certain situations, these materials can be used as weed barriers and then covered with wood chips or organic mulch. The problem is they can impede water penetration and gas exchange if they become too wet or too dry. The same goes if they're applied too heavily. Use no more than four to six sheets of newspaper or one layer of cardboard as sheet mulch.

Myth: Wood Chips Make the Best Mulch.

FACT: That depends on where you're using them. Wood chips are a wonderful mulch for a natural garden, but they hold too much moisture for cactuses and succulents. There are other caveats too. Don't spread them too heavily (no more than 3 inches thick) and don't pile them against plant stems—this can cause problems with bugs and rot.

BLACK WALNUT: BOSCHETTOPHOTOGRAPHY/GETTY IMAGES; SPADE, LAWN MOWER: BRAND X GARDEN IMAGES (2); VEGETABLE FACE: PASSAKORN VEJCHAYACHAI/SHUTTERSTOCK

Free Nitrogen

Myth: Leaving Grass Clippings on the Lawn Will Cause Thatch to Build Up.

FACT: Short grass clippings do not contribute to thatch—a thick layer of dead plant debris that makes it difficult for new turf to emerge. In fact, it's advised to leave your grass clippings in place, rather than bagging them, especially if you have a mulching mower. It's less work and the clippings are a free source of nitrogen for your lawn. For the best-looking grass, always keep lawn mower blades sharp.

Myth: The Reason Pepper Plants Aren't Setting Fruit Is Because the Soil Is Too Rich.

FACT: While overly rich soil will favor foliage over flowers, it won't stop pepper plants from bearing fruit altogether. It's more likely that a lack of flowering (and subsequent pepper production) is due to weather. A hot, drying wind will cause flowers to drop off. Also, many pepper plants are very temperature sensitive, so flowers will drop off below 55 degrees or above 85 degrees.

Early-Blooming Shrubs

Greet spring with pretty plants that shine all season

By Melinda Myers

DWARF RUSSIAN ALMOND: SKYMOON13/GETTY IMAGES

Fabulous Fruits

After its floral show, dwarf Russian almond produces nuts that are about ¾ inch long and have a hard, hairy shell.

‹ Dwarf Russian almond

PRUNUS TENELLA, ZONES 2 TO 6, SIZE: 2 TO 5 FEET TALL AND WIDE

This modest-sized shrub bookends the growing season with showy rose red spring flowers and yellow-orange fall color. It prefers full sun, tolerates a range of soil types and is fairly drought resistant. Ruth's 100 produces abundant blooms on a compact plant.

Why we love it: Flowers appear early and attract butterflies. Plus, the plant provides food and cover for backyard birds and wildlife.

^ Paperbush plant

EDGEWORTHIA CHRYSANTHA, ZONES 7 TO 9, SIZE: 3 TO 6 FEET TALL AND WIDER

Leafless stems provide interest in winter, while creamy yellow flowers with a spicy scent attract pollinators in late winter or early spring. The Gold Finch variety tolerates humidity and heat, and Grandiflora boasts larger flowers.

Why we love it: Dark green leaves turn rich yellow in fall, adding to its year-round appeal. And its bark can be used to make paper, hence its common name.

^ Bush cherry

PRUNUS JACQUEMONTII, ZONES 5 TO 8, SIZE: 5 FEET TALL AND WIDE

Here's a cherry that southern gardeners can also enjoy. Rose-colored buds open to fragrant pink flowers that attract butterflies and other pollinators. The green leaves are a larval host for the eastern tiger swallowtail butterfly and turn yellow in the fall. Grow these beauties in full sun with moist, well-draining soil.

Why we love it: The fruit, which ranges from red to plum purple, attracts birds to the landscape.

CORNELIAN CHERRY DOGWOOD: TOMTSYA/SHUTTERSTOCK

‹ Cornelian cherry dogwood

CORNUS MAS, ZONES 4 TO 8, SIZE: UP TO 20 FEET TALL AND WIDE

Welcome spring with bright yellow flowers that appear earlier than forsythia's blooms. It prefers full sun or part shade, and rich, moist, well-draining soil. Leaves turn purplish red in fall, and flaky bark adds winter interest.

Why we love it: The red fruits are edible, but they are tastier made into preserves, jellies and pies. Or leave them for the birds to enjoy.

^ Dwarf fothergilla

FOTHERGILLA GARDENII, ZONES 4 TO 9, SIZE: 3 TO 6 FEET TALL, 2 TO 6 FEET WIDE

The fothergilla is a slow grower that sends up additional shoots, forming a colony. Remove any unwanted stems to control its size. The blue-green leaves turn vibrant red, orange and yellow in the fall. Grow it in full sun to part shade, and in rich, moist, acidic soil.

Why we love it: White, honey-scented bottlebrush flowers attract bees and other beneficial pollinators.

^ Daphne

DAPHNE, ZONES 4 TO 8, SIZE: 6 INCHES TO 3 FEET TALL, 2 TO 3 FEET WIDE

Choose from a variety of sizes and spring bloom times. Grow in full sun to part shade where the lovely fragrant flowers can be enjoyed. Daphnes prefer moist, well-draining soil and protection from winter wind and sun.

Why we love it: The evergreen leaves of some cultivars and the variegated leaves of Carol Mackie make daphnes a welcome addition to a home garden of any size.

› Pearlbush

EXOCHORDA RACEMOSA, ZONES 4 TO 8, SIZE: UP TO 15 FEET TALL AND WIDE

Place this large shrub where you are sure to enjoy the spring floral display. Its pearl-like flower buds open into white flowers in midspring, followed by interesting seed capsules. Use it as a hedge or include it in a mixed or shrub border. Prune immediately after blooming for best results.

Why we love it: Growing in full sun to part shade, this shrub is low maintenance as well as heat and drought tolerant.

DWARF FOTHERGILLA, DAPHNE: BAILEY NURSERIES (2); PEARLBUSH: COURTESY OF PROVEN WINNERS – WWW.PROVENWINNERS.COM;

^ Vernal witch hazel

HAMAMELIS VERNALIS, ZONES 4 TO 8, SIZE: 6 TO 10 FEET TALL AND WIDER

Enjoy seasons of color from this North American native. Fragrant flowers are golden yellow, orange or burgundy-red. Leaves emerge reddish bronze, turn green in summer and shift to yellow in fall. The best flowering happens in full sun, but the plant tolerates part shade.

Why we love it: This beauty attracts songbirds, but deer leave it alone.

^ Flowering quince

CHAENOMELES SPECIOSA, ZONES 4 TO 9, SIZE: 6 TO 10 FEET TALL AND WIDE

Quince's white, pink or red flowers are followed by an apple-like fruit that turns yellow in the fall (make it into preserves and jellies). Leaves emerge a bronzy red before turning green in summer. Grow in full sun for the best flowering.

Why we love it: The colorful flowers attract butterflies and hummingbirds.

‹ Japanese pieris

PIERIS JAPONICA, ZONES 4 TO 7, SIZE: 9 TO 12 FEET TALL, 6 TO 8 FEET WIDE

Grow as a large shrub or small tree in full sun to part shade. It prefers moist, well-draining, acidic soil, as well as a location where its evergreen leaves are protected from winter winds.

Why we love it: The showy buds that form in late summer add beauty to the winter garden before opening into flowers in early spring.

Garden Center Buying Tips You Need to Know

Get thrifty during your next shopping excursion with these helpful reader recommendations

Find out what day the plant vendors deliver. They pull plants and put them in the markdown area to make room for new arrivals. I've had great success with this.

Doreen Damm NEW PORT RICHEY, FL

Buying plants out of blooming season will save you money, but you'll have to wait until the following year to enjoy them.

Carole A. Reis FELTON, CA

I always get to know the staff at the garden center. They give me advice about caring for plants in my region, when plants will go on sale and more.

Glenda Ferguson PAOLI, IN

Go prepared. Take pictures of your planting area, know how much sun and shade there is, decide how much time you are willing to spend on maintenance and, most importantly, know what size you want the mature plants to be.

Kathy Eppers ALEDO, TX

Purchase common species at big-box stores, then splurge at local nurseries on more unusual plants.

Gerry Hofmann FORT COLLINS, CO

Ask for a discount if a bag is ripped or a plant looks shabby.

Joan Heid CHESTER, SC

TOP: AKARAWUT/SHUTTERSTOCK; BOTTOM: PRANEE MANKIT/GETTY IMAGES

What's Your Best Gardening Hack?

Readers offer tips and tricks for getting the most out of favorite backyard activities

I mapped out my garden and identified the location of all my plants. If I'm not sure whether something's a weed or plant, I'll use a plant identification app to verify before I pull it out.

Boni Trombetta WEST CHESTER, PA

Planting ground covers helps me avoid extra work, such as mulching or weeding, in the long run.

Juli Seyfried CINCINNATI, OH

I can grow an abundance of tomatoes, but not zucchini, so I put in extra varieties of tomatoes for trading with my zucchini-growing friends.

Rebecca Williamson BUSHNELL, IL

Red barrenwort is a low-maintenance ground cover.

Heirloom tomatoes

I use an auger with my drill to dig holes for bulbs.

Karen Hance NORTH TONAWANDA, NY

Melons tend to ripen faster and taste sweeter when you elevate them on small upside-down tin cans. This keeps them off the cool ground and lets them soak up more heat from the sun.

Sue Gronholz BEAVER DAM, WI

I make my own fertilizer by boiling and baking old eggshells until dry. Then I grind them into a fine powder with my food processor.

Jennifer Broadstreet Hess MARION, KS

Save the Rain

How you can put excess water to good use in your garden or landscaping

By Erica Browne Grivas

Your saved rainwater can be used to irrigate trees, shrubs and flower beds.

RAIN BARRELS ARE CONTAINERS DESIGNED TO capture and hold rainwater for later use in gardens and landscaping. Using a rain barrel can lower your water bill, help reduce stormwater runoff and enhance the health of your local environment. Here's what you need to know to get started.

The Benefits

Out in nature, a large amount of rain is absorbed directly back into the ground, replenishing the soil, and the rest either evaporates or is runoff that ends up in creeks, rivers, lakes or other bodies of water. But that amount drops significantly in more developed areas.

Rain barrels can help prevent stormwater from overwhelming storm sewers and lessen groundwater pollution and flooding during heavy rain events.

"A major benefit is having free water on-site and easy to access, while reducing how much water is running off," says Laura Matter, a horticulturist for over 40 years. Based in Seattle, Washington, Laura leads the Natural Yard Care program for Tilth Alliance, a nonprofit working with "farmers, gardeners and eaters to build a sustainable, healthy and equitable food future."

As rainwater picks up pollutants on roofs and roadways, "excess water in storm drains can be a problem in sewers, which can be connected to surrounding water bodies," Laura says.

Several cities and government agencies offer incentives for rain barrels (and other rain-harvesting tools) to encourage water conservation. Consult your local city, public utilities and water district websites for the latest on potential rebate programs or restrictions, as some states or counties have specific rules for collecting water.

How to Collect

Rain barrels are typically positioned under a downspout to capture water from your roof. Depending on your climate, roof size and water needs, you may want to gather more water than an average 55-gallon rain barrel can hold.

"That isn't going to get you through the summer," says Laura. One option is to link several barrels in a chain that fills up in succession. For a large property, consider a tank or cistern.

You'll want to check your roof material before setting up a rain barrel. Some materials, such as asphalt shingles, treated wood, copper, PVC or zinc panels can leach metals and toxic materials into the water. In those cases, look into other options, such as tanks that collect rain that hasn't touched the roof.

LEFT: STANLEY45/GETTY IMAGES; RIGHT, CLOCKWISE FROM TOP LEFT: RAIN WATER SOLUTIONS,

Top Picks

1 This sleek 50-gallon design (*wayfair.com*) made of recycled materials will fit in urban yards and easily connect to other barrels, and it is opaque so as to discourage algae.

2 Holding 90 gallons of rainwater, this plastic rain barrel from Good Ideas (*wayfair.com*) has an overflow-friendly top with a planter feature that's the perfect setting for a plant.

3 This teardrop-shaped rain barrel (*gardeners.com*) is made out of polyethylene, which is resistant to both chipping and UV light. Plus it comes with a 5-foot hose and holds 65 gallons of rainwater.

Your saved rainwater can be used to irrigate trees, shrubs and flower beds; feed into a rain garden; or wash your home or car. Because roof water can contain particulates from birds, moss and roof tile materials, it's not recommended to use it for drinking or for watering edible plants.

Be sure to keep the filters clean and drain the container before freezing temperatures arrive if your barrel isn't winter-proof.

What to Look For

In addition to sturdy construction and fittings that can withstand your local heat and cold extremes, experts recommend looking for a rain barrel that:

- has a filter to keep away bugs, especially mosquitoes.
- has a child- and animal-proof lid that closes firmly or locks.
- is made of food-safe materials.
- provides easy access to the water.
- has an overflow hose to keep excess water away from your home.
- has a spigot low on the barrel to limit water stagnation.
- can be elevated for gravity-fed irrigation or linked to other barrels if needed.

How Do You Save Water in the Garden?

Readers share their inventive ways of keeping plants happy without turning the spigot

Reuse rain barrel water collected from clean and maintained roofs.

I haven't hooked up my garden hose for years. Instead, I catch excess water with a bucket in my shower, capture condensation from my air conditioner and save water from when I wash my produce.

Lois Brumfield PORTLAND, OR

Letting my garden dry out during the day, then soaking the soil in the evening reduces evaporation.

Ken Orich LETHBRIDGE, AB

Recycled water from a dehumidifier helps me water my plants.

Nikki Conell WILLOUGHBY, OH

When I fill the kiddie pool for my grandchildren, I don't dump it out after. Instead, I fill all my watering cans and buckets with the leftover water.

Kathleen Norton WESTMINSTER, MA

I sprinkle each plant individually and deeply instead of mass drenching my gardens to save water.

Charlotte Estabrook SIGNAL MOUNTAIN, TN

I have three rain barrels that I use all spring and summer to water my ornamental garden plants, to fill the birdbaths and fountains, and sometimes even to wash my hair!

Anita Allen TIRO, OH

MALINIKART/ALAMY STOCK PHOTO

Under the Surface

Facts about earthworms, complex garden visitors

By Christine Peterson

1,000,000 An acre of soil may be home to more than 1,000,000 earthworms when soil conditions are ideal.

6 Australia's giant Gippsland earthworm can grow up to 6 feet long, making it one of the longest in the world.

1/2 Earthworms, which do have mouths but not teeth, may consume around half their body weight in a day.

7,000 Researchers have discovered an estimated 7,000 species of earthworms around the world—but it's likely that even more exist.

0 Zero native earthworms live in certain parts of the northern U.S., and nonnative species pose a threat to some North American landscapes and forest ecosystems.

6-8 In certain cases, earthworms may live six to eight years (though fewer is likely).

MALINIKART/ALAMY STOCK PHOTO

Herbaceous Homes

A step-by-step guide to growing your favorite herbs in a container

By Wendy Helfenbaum

GROWING HERBS IN CONTAINERS HAS ITS PERKS, both in the kitchen and the garden. In fact, it's easier to grow herbs in pots than in the ground, because you have more control of what's going on in the container, says Sue Goetz, a garden designer and author of *Complete Container Herb Gardening*.

"What I love about container gardening with herbs is that you can put them anywhere—on a balcony, patio or windowsill, or keep them tucked in a corner of the yard," Sue says. She also notes that pots just outside the kitchen offer easy access to fresh herbs while you're cooking.

Choose Your Greens

Only select herbs you want to cook with. "Grow what you love. If you don't use sage, you're not going to want it taking up space," Sue says.

Because some herbs such as sage, lavender, rosemary and thyme tend to germinate slowly, purchase seedling plants from your local nursery, Sue suggests.

"For herbs that are easy to grow, such as chives, basil and parsley, you can start with seeds, but I like the instant gratification of a plant," she says.

Find the Perfect Pot

When picking a container, you have many options. Choose any vessel that fits the style of your garden or home. Just make sure there are drainage holes in the bottom.

"I love to put herbs in terra cotta, but you can use glazed pots, fun galvanized metal containers or plastic," Sue says. You can also use fabric planters, which come in several sizes.

Plant in Good Soil

"Start with a really good-quality potting soil, because it's well-draining and nutritious," says Sue, who prefers organic potting soil and an occasional dose of liquid fertilizer. Garden soil compacts too quickly in pots, which reduces soil drainage.

Stay Sunny

Most herbs need six to eight hours of full sun to thrive. Read the plant label or seed packet carefully for success.

"The real bonus of containers is that if there's a part in the garden that's shady, you can always scoot the planter off the patio and into more sun," Sue says.

Just Add Water

Sue adds that gardeners should only water herbs when the soil is dry. Poke a finger about an inch into the soil to gauge the moisture.

Your plants' moisture needs depend on the kind of pot. "Clay terra-cotta pots dry out faster, so you may need to water those every day, while plastic ones don't lose water as fast, so maybe it's every couple of days," Sue says. Once you get into a watering rhythm, it will be no time until your first harvest.

Basil

Healthy Harvest

Frequent harvesting promotes fresh growth. Use your fingers to pinch off sprigs of chives, parsley, cilantro or basil. Herb snips work for basil, parsley and dill, and for woody herbs such as oregano or thyme. For large clumps of herbs, use pruning shears. Harvest foliage herbs such as oregano or basil before they flower, clipping them in the morning when they have the most flavor.

Herbs for Beginners

- Basil
- Chives
- Cilantro
- Dill
- Lemon balm
- Mint
- Oregano
- Parsley
- Sage
- Thyme

LEFT: WESTEND61; RIGHT: DARWEL; ILLUSTRATIONS: SPICYTRUFFEL/GETTY IMAGES (3)

Daffodil

Hyacinth

Tulip

Bearded iris

Canna lily

Mint

True Bulb

True bulbs (in other words, they are not rhizomes, corms or tubers) contain a plant's bud, stem and leaves inside a compact unit with layers that resemble the inside of an onion.

Rhizome

This type of stem structure has the ability to stretch underground horizontally. Some invasive plants and weeds spread out via rhizomes to quickly dominate a landscape.

Bulbs & Beyond

Take a closer look at four types of plant producers

Anemone

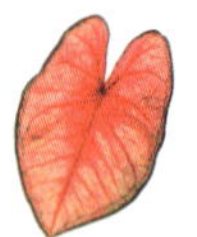
Caladium

Oxalis

Crocus

Freesia

Gladiolus

Tuber

The best-known tubers are potatoes. Tubers are underground stems and can bud from multiple spots. They can be divided to grow more.

Corm

Corm resembles true bulbs but is a solid unit of tissue, unlike a bulb's layers of developing leaves. New corms often grow on top of spent ones.

TULIP BULB, OXALIS, FREESIA: IBULB (3); DAFFODIL, HYACINTH, IRIS, CROCUS: COURTESY BRECK'S BULB CO. (4); TULIP, ANEMONE: BALL HORTICULTURAL COMPANY (2); RHIZOME: KHORZHEVSKA/SHUTTERSTOCK; CANNA LILY, CALADIUM:

How to Deter Chipmunks or Groundhogs?

Home gardeners share favorite techniques for keeping certain critters away

I try to find the groundhog's home (usually under my shed or deck) and have used a floodlight and music as a deterrent under the deck. I'm not sure which worked, but the groundhog and its family left.

Boni Trombetta WEST CHESTER, PA

To keep chipmunks from eating the roots of my potted plants, I put small flat stones on top of the soil.

Monica Partington RALEIGH, NC

I don't! I adore and welcome them to my yard.

Kathleen Delaney JAMESTOWN, NY

Chipmunk

Groundhog

Vinegar can help keep away critters. You have to apply it often enough that the scent stays detectable by humans (and therefore stronger to the animals).

Kathryn Rucci ORLANDO, FL

I scatter my husband's hair around the garden after giving him a cut.

Char Jasinski NEW BERLIN, WI

To prevent them from eating my lettuce, carrot tops, beet greens and more, I make hoops and cover them with bird netting. They get the hint!

Sue Gronholz BEAVER DAM, WI

GROUNDHOG: SHANNON BUTTERFIELD/500PX; ROCK PILE: ALXPIN/GETTY IMAGES (2); CHIPMUNK: DIANE MARSHMAN

What Your Rose Is Saying

Five signs your shrub needs your help

By Erica Browne Grivas

At Last rose

IT'S CHALLENGING TO DIAGNOSE THE VISUAL irregularities on your roses. Use these clues from garden pros to get started with a diagnosis.

If Your Rose:

Grows rampant with few flowers

It Could Need:

Pruning

For modern shrub and hybrid tea roses, simple pruning—best done before leaves emerge—promotes air circulation, bushy growth and lusty flowering.

"A rose is just a blooming shrub, and you can treat it as that," says Teresa Byington, a consulting rosarian for the American Rose Society, who gardens in Indiana. For these types, the typical timing cue, she says, is when forsythia is blooming.

Remove dead, broken, crossing or diseased canes, and take down the rest by one-third of the plant's height, she says. This encourages healthy growth. Single-blooming heirloom and species roses can be pruned for shape and deadheading after blooming, and climbers have their own regimen.

If Your Rose:

Produces hard seed heads

Do This:

Leave for the birds or make tea

Rose hips are the fruit that roses produce after flowering. They have up to 20 times the vitamin C of an orange and add a floral note to teas. Rose hips look stunning in fall arrangements, and birds love to snack on them.

Teresa recommends deadheading flowers until about six weeks before your first frost date, and then let hips form to help the plant prepare for winter.

AT LAST, OSO EASY PAPRIKA: WWW.PROVENWINNERS.COM (2); DOWNY MILDEW: ZOONAR GMBH/ALAMY STOCK PHOTO

Oso Easy
Paprika rose

If Your Rose:
Develops black spots on the leaves

It Could Be:
Black spot
"Black spot is a fungal disease that's spread in water when leaves are wet. It usually starts at the plant's base and works upward," says Stephen Scanniello, curator of the Peggy Rockefeller Rose Garden at the New York Botanical Garden and author of two rose books.

Black spot disease will defoliate—but not kill—the plant. Allowing ventilation through pruning and plant spacing is key, as is removing the affected foliage to prevent the spread of the fungus, he says.

If Your Rose:
Exhibits significant yellowing or dropping of leaves

It Could Be:
Soil issues
"Usually underwatering and overwatering have the same symptoms," Stephen says. "Any kind of sudden leaf drop or leaves turning yellow indicates something is wrong with the soil, such as lack of drainage or chlorosis, which is a lack of iron." He recommends regular soil testing to learn what's happening before addressing any issues.

If Your Rose:
Has gangly new growth and a different flower

It Could Be:
Graft issues
In this case, the rootstock variety has taken over your grafted rose and is reaching for the sky. These vigorous shoots can sap energy from the desired variety. You can buy own-root roses, which are typically hardier, but on grafted roses they bury the knobby union 2 inches below the surface, Teresa says.

Disease Cues
Hints that your rose may be sick:

1 Red stains and/or bumps on the canes

2 Broom growth or thick canes with clustered thorns

3 Fuzzy white patches or spots on leaves

1. *Downy mildew.*
2. *Rose rosette disease,* which is contagious. Dispose of plants and report to *roserosette.org/reporting.*
3. *Powdery mildew.*

ROSETTE DISEASE: SUSAN VINEYARD/ALAMY STOCK PHOTO; POWDERY MILDEW: IMAGEBROKER/ALAMY STOCK PHOTO

What Is Your Best Rose-Growing Tip?

Discover the innovative garden hacks that readers use to encourage healthy blooms

Rainbow Sorbet rose

I've loved tending to my 27 rose bushes. To prevent rose cane borers, I dab some liquid wood glue on the tip of cane cuts so that the insects won't enter the cane through a wound.

Sandra Nehls WATERTOWN, WI

Roses like to be well-watered, so make sure to apply a layer of mulch to retain moisture.

Kathy Eppers ALEDO, TX

Nourish roses with love and enjoy them often, which will alert you early if there are any problems.

Gloria Durman KENT, OH

Create a schedule for inspecting, deadheading, watering, feeding, applying treatments (if needed) and pruning. And then stick to it. Consistency is my best tip.

Joanne Thomas BAYONNE, NJ

Never give up on roses, even if they look dead.

Stephanie Caron LUCEDALE, MS

Take time to sanitize your pruning shears after each use. That's how I prevent fungal disease in my rose garden.

Jennifer Broadstreet Hess MARION, KS

How Do You Support Pollinators?

Readers share how they make outdoor spaces welcoming to butterflies, bees and more

It was my goal to create a backyard bird, bee and butterfly haven. To achieve this, I planted bee balm, coneflowers, beautyberry, phlox, butterfly weed and more. I also have potted hibiscus and lantana.

Mary Willmuth LITTLE ROCK, AR

We have a 7-foot Joe Pye weed that is a magnet for bees and butterflies.

Cheryl Rogan HOFFMAN ESTATES, IL

My entire front yard, about a half acre, is full of wildflowers.

Debbie Foote ST. JOHNS, MI

Cosmos and larkspur

Monarch on milkweed

I plant some prairie natives and host plants for caterpillars, including milkweed for monarchs and dill and fennel for black swallowtails.

Eva Bellinger SUN PRAIRIE, WI

Honeybees moved into a tree's cavity near my house. I'm allergic, so I worked with a beekeeper and tree cutter to safely relocate the bees.

Cindi Gordon MADISONVILLE, TN

I'm fortunate to keep two beehives at an organic farm to help pollinate the crops. In return, I get some delicious honey.

Robert Lister LIMINGTON, ME

Busy Bees

Fuzzy, gentle and efficient, mason bees are champion pollinators. Here's why you want to attract them to your garden.

By Amy Grisak

Mason bees, like this male that just emerged from a cocoon, are very nonaggressive.

MORE THAN 150 SPECIES MAKE UP a group of native bees called mason bees, which handled pollination here in the U.S. long before European honeybees entered the picture.

"Solitary bees such as mason bees are perfectly adapted for great pollination," says Matthew Shepherd, director of outreach and education for the Xerces Society for Invertebrate Conservation.

Unlike honeybees that gather pollen in packages on their hind legs, mason bees belly-flop into blossoms, and the pollen clings to the hairs on their bodies. As a result, they can pollinate up to 2,000 flowers per day, according to Thyra McKelvie of Rent Mason Bees in Bothell, Washington. She also notes that each mason bee can do the work of 100 honeybees. And because they're well-adapted to the climate, they fly in cooler temperatures and brave drizzly conditions.

Gentle Gardeners

The busy fliers are valuable in home gardens because they pollinate an array of early-blooming plants. Plus, they're easy to raise and fun to watch.

Renowned for their gentle disposition, mason bees are suitable for families with children and are not aggressive even in close proximity. Male mason bees do not sting. And about the only way to incite a defensive sting from a female is to squeeze or step on her.

The reason for this docility is their lifestyle. Thyra notes that mason bees do not have hives, so there's nothing to defend. "Their life cycle is similar to a butterfly," she says. While a honeybee queen lays 1,500 to 2,000 eggs per day, a female mason bee produces only 15 in her four- to six-week lifetime.

A female blue mason bee gathers pollen from a plum tree blossom and adds it to the scopa, the area under her abdomen that holds pollen.

Instead of laying eggs in honeycomb cells, mason bees use existing gaps or tunnels. A female creates a mud plug on one end, adds a loaf of pollen and nectar, then lays an egg. The next layer follows the same pattern until the tunnel is packed with eggs and sealed with more mud. Hence the name "mason" bee.

Once the eggs hatch, each larva consumes its pollen loaf and spins a silken, hardened cocoon to overwinter in. Young mason bees emerge when conditions warm in spring. The males (noted by the white tuft of fuzz on their heads) appear first, with females appearing soon after.

Bee a Good Host

Creating an ideal environment for these bees is critical. "All bees need habitat," Matthew says. He recommends planting flowers (particularly native varieties), avoiding pesticides and creating nest sites. You can provide nesting tubes or allow a certain level of "imperfection" in your yard and garden. For example, mason bees may use chambers in dead trees where birds have pecked holes to find insects.

Hosting these gentle, highly efficient and low-maintenance bees is a perfect way to encourage pollinators and help protect their population. Welcome them to your garden during spring and see what all the buzz is about.

Pollinators for Rent

Temporarily host these friendly fliers with a bee house from Rent Mason Bees.

It's simple! You order a kit (which includes bees) to arrive in early spring. When the bees are done pollinating your yard, mail back the nesting block. Rent Mason Bees harvests, cleans and protects the cocoons over the winter and then provides bees to farmers and gardeners, who release them into their crops. For more information, visit *rentmasonbees.com*.

Bordered patch butterfly on firewheel

9 Ways to Attract Butterflies

Make your garden the most popular stop around with expert tips and tricks

By Jill Staake

Gulf fritillary on smooth beggarticks

Painted lady on buttonbush

ANYONE CAN FILL A GARDEN WITH the vivid colors of delicate butterflies. Jaret Daniels, author of multiple butterfly field guides and associate professor at the McGuire Center for Lepidoptera at the University of Florida's Museum of Natural History, offers his advice for getting more visitors.

1. Grow Local

Native plants are the perfect choice for a butterfly garden. "They are adapted to the local soils and climate," Jaret says. "As a result, they often perform better than nonnative species." You'll spend less money and effort to attract more butterflies in the long run.

"Natives often have the reputation of looking unkempt or weedy," Jaret says. "But there are many natives that are just as attractive as nonnative ornamentals." Visit a native plant nursery or contact your local county extension office to get a good list for your area.

2. Start with Nectar Favorites

Jaret recommends putting in a selection of popular nectar plants, then getting a good field guide to learn which butterfly species visit them the most. But don't go crazy and buy one of everything you see.

Black swallowtail emerging from chrysalis

Sunflowers provide nectar for butterflies, such as monarchs, and seeds for birds.

Monarch caterpillars on butterfly weed

"The kid-in-a-candy-store approach may not yield the best results," says Jaret. "Instead, select several really good plants and buy a few of each. The larger waves of color help draw in insects." Include plants of varying heights, and don't neglect shady spots—some butterflies prefer them.

3. Add Host Plants

Once you've identified the butterflies visiting your backyard, add the host plants that their caterpillars need. Each species has its own set of requirements. For instance, monarchs use milkweed, while eastern black swallowtails eat from the parsley family. Once again, natives reign supreme, so consider choosing local species of milkweed and other hosts for the most success.

FIRST SPREAD: ROLF NUSSBAUMER; SECOND SPREAD, CLOCKWISE FROM LEFT: LAWRENCE JEFFERSON/SHUTTERSTOCK;

4. Create a Caterpillar Haven

It usually takes about two weeks for a caterpillar to reach full size. Then it spends 10 to 14 days as a chrysalis before emerging as a butterfly. "Most adult butterflies live only a few short weeks," Jaret says. "The other life stages actually reside in your garden much longer, and are just as attractive and entertaining."

Of course, all butterfly gardeners should avoid using pesticides altogether. Find alternative ways to deal with true pests, such as picking them off by hand, which helps keep caterpillars safe.

5. Offer Shelter

A butterfly weighs about as much as a paper clip, so to them a raindrop can feel like a bowling ball. They seek shelter in bad weather and overnight, often in shrubbery or ornamental grasses, or tucked into cracks in rock piles. Provide these spaces for extra security.

6. Treasure Your Trees

You may picture sunny meadows when thinking of butterflies, but plenty of species, such as red-spotted purples and white admirals, prefer shade. In spring, running tree sap provides some of the earliest butterfly meals. A few trees serve as host plants too. For example, tiger swallowtail caterpillars use cottonwood, birch and black cherry trees as nurseries.

7. Serve Sweets

Many butterflies enjoy fruit in addition to (or instead of) nectar from flowers. Grow native berry-producing shrubs or fruit trees, allowing the fruit to drop to the ground naturally. As it rots, the fruit becomes a draw for species such as red admirals and mourning cloaks. If you see a lot of fruit lovers, try setting out a plate of overripe bananas or juicy options such as oranges or watermelon. Beware—this can also attract raccoons and other pests, so bring the fruit plate in at night.

8. Protect Puddles

Male butterflies like to cluster on mud puddles (or you may find them on animal dung or roadkill), where they glean valuable salts and minerals. It's hard to create these spots artificially, so if you have a popular muddy area in your garden, leave it be. The butterflies will thank you.

9. Appreciate Your Space

Whether you have a huge lot or a tiny balcony, you can attract butterflies. "A butterfly garden can be any size," says Jaret. "Small beds or container gardens with a combination of colorful nectar plants and a larval host plant or two can be quite effective."

Attract black swallowtails with drought-tolerant yellow coneflowers.

Jaret shares a final thought: "My theme for the past few years has been 'all landscapes matter.' With habitat loss, the landscapes that we as humans manage every day are increasingly important to wildlife. So the choices we make in our home gardens really matter."

BELETSKIY_NIKOLAY/SHUTTERSTOCK; IRINAK/SHUTTERSTOCK; THIS SPREAD, CLOCKWISE FROM TOP LEFT: SYLVIA GUARINO; KEVIN COLLISON/SHUTTERSTOCK; JIM MCKINLEY/GETTY IMAGES

Whimsical Perennials

Add easy-care flowers to create a cottage garden style

By Niki Jabbour

VIOLET PROFUSION SALVIA, CAT'S MEOW CATMINT, BANANA CREAM SHASTA DAISY: COURTESY OF PROVEN WINNERS – WWW.

‹ Violet Profusion salvia

SALVIA NEMOROSA, ZONES 3 TO 8

Add a bold pop of purple with this fragrant and wildlife-friendly salvia. This compact perennial tops out at 16 inches tall and 20 inches wide and makes an eye-catching edge along a pathway, fence or garden bed.

Why we love it: As a reblooming salvia, it can produce a second burst of purple flowers in early autumn. Shear back the plants after the first floral fade to encourage a quick turnaround.

^ Moonbeam threadleaf coreopsis

COREOPSIS VERTICILLATA, ZONES 3 TO 9

Also called tickseed, this compact plant sold by Monrovia has lacy foliage and grows up to 18 inches tall and 24 inches wide. By early summer the plants are smothered in lemon yellow daisylike flowers that persist for months. For constant blooms, gently shear it after its first flowers fade.

Why we love it: It's an award-winning perennial that is long-lived and easy to grow.

^ Cat's Meow catmint

NEPETA FAASSENII, ZONES 3 TO 8

A perfect perennial for a flower border, this colorful bloomer grows up to 20 inches tall and 36 inches wide. Unlike most catmint types, which tend to flop, this selection has tidy, upright growth. Its purple flower spikes last from early summer through autumn, attracting bees, butterflies and hummingbirds.

Why we love it: Catmint is drought tolerant and resistant to grazing from deer and rabbits.

‹ Banana Cream Shasta daisy

LEUCANTHEMUM SUPERBUM, ZONES 5 TO 9

This daisy has massive yellow blooms that mature to a creamy white, resulting in a multicolored display in spring and summer. It is up to 18 inches tall and 24 inches wide, and it makes a great border or container plant.

Why we love it: One of the biggest benefits of planting a cottage garden is cutting flowers for bouquets. These Shasta daisy blooms last at least two weeks in a vase.

^ Blue Fortune anise hyssop

AGASTACHE, ZONES 4 TO 9

This multipurpose perennial checks all the boxes—it's pest resistant and drought tolerant, and it flowers for months, producing clouds of pale lavender blooms. Pair it with rudbeckia or purple coneflower for an impressive late-summer display.

Why we love it: Its leaves and flowers have the fragrance and flavor of black licorice. Steep them for an aromatic cup of tea, or add them to salads and smoothies.

^ Gay Butterflies butterfly weed

ASCLEPIAS TUBEROSA, ZONES 4 TO 11

Welcome butterflies and bees to your cottage garden with several clumps of this low-care perennial that's both drought tolerant and pest resistant. Sold by Monrovia, this plant showcases blooms from mid- to late summer with fiery gold, yellow and scarlet flower clusters.

Why we love it: Butterfly weed is a species of milkweed, which is the only type of host plant for monarch butterflies.

› Perfectly Picasso speedwell

VERONICA LONGIFOLIA, ZONES 4 TO 9

Paint the garden pretty with the bubblegum pink flowers of this pollinator-friendly perennial that grows 2 feet tall and wide. Its graceful, dense flower spikes put on a show for up to six weeks beginning in midsummer. The blooms also make long-lived cut flowers.

Why we love it: The slender flower spikes bloom from the bottom up, creating a striking two-toned appearance.

BLUE FORTUNE ANISE HYSSOP, PERFECTLY PICASSO SPEEDWELL: WALTERS GARDENS, INC (2); GAY BUTTERFLIES BUTTERFLY WEED: DOREEN WYNJA FOR MONROVIA; RASPBERRY WINE BEE BALM:

^ David garden phlox

PHLOX PANICULATA, ZONES 4 TO 8

Reliable, long flowering and disease resistant, this phlox is an outstanding choice. Plants grow up to 4 feet tall, with strong stems topped with large clusters of fragrant white blooms. Unlike other cultivars, David offers excellent resistance to powdery mildew.

Why we love it: This summer staple is extremely vigorous, and its nectar-rich flowers entice hummingbirds and butterflies to the garden.

^ Raspberry Wine bee balm

MONARDA DIDYMA, ZONES 4 TO 9

Bee balm is a classic plant beloved by cottage gardeners, as well as hummingbirds and bees. This bold cultivar with aromatic foliage boasts masses of raspberry red blossoms. With plants that grow 2 to 3 feet tall and wide, it's perfect for both large and small gardens.

Why we love it: This is a low-maintenance perennial species and is resistant to deer and powdery mildew.

‹ Tangerine Dream coneflower

ECHINACEA, ZONES 4 TO 9

This sun-loving coneflower with a honey scent lights up the summer garden with large bright orange flowers. The compact beauty grows up to 2 feet tall and wide.

Why we love it: Coneflowers are pollinator magnets. Once the flowers fade, the seed heads feed birds such as goldfinches and blue jays.

Taking On Invasives

Tips for identifying, removing and replacing problematic plants

By Melinda Myers

Certain invasives, such as this purple loosestrife, look beautiful but can create big garden problems.

FROM LEFT: MAGICFLUTE002, MARTHA SNIDER/GETTY IMAGES (2); CALIN TATU/SHUTTERSTOCK

Kudzu

Japanese honeysuckle

THE TAG AT THE GARDEN center may say that a plant is "long blooming, low maintenance and fast growing." If this description seems too good to be true, it's because it sometimes is. Many plants once recommended for the garden have since left our carefully curated landscapes and invaded nearby natural areas. Once invasive plants gain a foothold in natural spaces, they crowd out the native plants that birds, pollinators and other wildlife depend upon.

Invasives are defined as nonnative, adaptable plants that reproduce by seeds, stems and roots, which are either spread by wind, deposited by birds or carried into new areas by people, pets and visiting wildlife.

Buy Suitable Plants

To avoid accidentally adding troublesome plants to your yard, do a bit of research before purchasing. Check with your local nature center, the Department of Natural Resources or a nearby university extension service for lists of invasive species in your region. In addition, the United States Forest Service (*fs.usda.gov*) and Invasive Plant Atlas of the United States (*invasiveplantatlas.org*) are two other helpful online resources.

Pay Attention to Decor

Door swags and wreaths can also contribute to this problem. These decorations can contain invasive plants, such as teasel and oriental bittersweet. Their seeds are released from the arrangements into nearby gardens, eventually making their way to natural spaces.

Get Rid of Tick Havens

Removing invasive plants also can help reduce disease-carrying tick populations. Studies have found that the presence of Japanese barberry and honeysuckle bushes create the perfect habitat for both deer and the ticks that feed on them.

Weed Them Out

Remove and discard small invasive plants, including the roots, as recommended by your local municipality. Many allow you to place these in the trash since they will be buried in a landfill. Avoid composting invasive plants unless your pile is hot enough (150 to 180 degrees) to kill the plants, roots and seeds.

You will need to use different techniques for larger tree and shrub specimens. You can slowly kill problem trees by either removing a 6-inch strip of bark around the base of the plant or painting the bottom 12 inches of the trunk with a recommended herbicide. You can also choose to cut the plant to the ground, then treat the stump with either a brush or total vegetation killer to prevent the stump and roots from sprouting. As always, read and follow label directions carefully.

Add Natives Instead

Have fun replacing troublemaking plants with better alternatives. Select native plants suited to your backyard's growing conditions and available space and, of course, look for options that support birds and pollinators.

Most Common Invasives

- Barberries
- Buckthorn
- Chinese and Japanese wisterias
- English ivy
- Garlic mustard
- Japanese honeysuckle
- Japanese knotweed
- Kudzu
- Oriental bittersweet
- Purple loosestrife
- Queen Anne's lace
- Tree-of-heaven

Space Invaders

Hard facts on invasive plants and their effects

By Jill Staake

Purple loosestrife

Russian thistle

TOP RIGHT: EUGENY POPOV/SHUTTERSTOCK; TOP LEFT AND BOTTOM: TOM MEAKER, DANUT VIERU/GETTY IMAGES (2)

1873 **Russian thistle, better known as tumbleweed, accidentally came to the U.S. in 1873 and spread rapidly. Today, it infests approximately 100 million acres, especially in the American Southwest.**

2 An invasive plant has two characteristics: First, it is nonnative to the ecosystem, and second, it causes or is likely to cause harm to humans, the environment or the economy.

159 The invasive aquatic plant *Elodea*, which chokes out native vegetation, could cost the Alaskan sockeye salmon industry as much as $159 million a year.

500 Himalayan blackberry is invasive in the Pacific Northwest, forming impenetrable thickets of up to 500 canes per square yard.

2.7 A single invasive purple loosestrife plant can produce more than 2.7 million seeds annually.

5 Giant hogweed's leaves grow up to 5 feet across. Its toxic sap causes severe skin blisters when exposed to sunlight.

1 In summer, kudzu vine can grow up to 1 foot every day, reaching lengths of over 100 feet.

Himalayan blackberry

Berry Secrets

Surprising facts about the juicy fruits you love

By Peggy Riccio

1966

It was illegal to grow currants and gooseberries in the U.S. until 1966. They were hosts to white pine blister rust, a fungus that destroys white pine trees. Some states still have restrictions in place, and growing these berries may require a special permit.

2 Blackberries are available only in the color black, but they come in two forms: with and without thorns.

1 Botanically, a banana is a berry because it is produced from an individual flower containing one ovary. Modern cultivars are seedless.

4 Raspberry fruits come in four colors: red, black, purple and gold.

4-5 Blueberries prefer soil as acidic as 4 to 5 pH. You may need to test your soil for guidance on adjusting your pH before you plant blueberries.

200 Every strawberry has an average of 200 seeds, found on the outside of the fruit.

30 Elderberry shrubs are known to feed more than 30 bird species, such as cedar waxwings, northern mockingbirds and gray catbirds. Plus, they provide shelter and nest sites.

TOP AND BOTTOM: SHANA NOVAK, T_KIMURA/GETTY IMAGES (2)

Combine double impatiens, sweet potato vine and coleus for a colorful display.

Small-Space Wonders

Design and create baskets brimming with gorgeous blooms and foliage

By Wendy Helfenbaum

TO DISPLAY A LOT OF COLOR in a small space, just look up. Hanging baskets can expand your garden and add interest to decks, patios and porches. Building your own is fun and offers more options, says Brooke Edmunds, a community horticulturist with Oregon State University. Here's how to create showstopping hanging baskets from start to finish.

1. Choose Your Container

Baskets come in many sizes and styles. Select a basket material that's lightweight, such as wire, plastic, wicker or peat.

"You can get creative and reuse something too," says Brooke. Metal watering cans, colanders and other containers can also work if they have drainage holes or if you add them yourself.

When picking the container size, keep in mind what you plan on growing. A basket that's too small for your plants requires more watering and pruning. For larger plants with deep root systems, a bigger basket offers more depth and soil surface. Baskets with open sides will allow you to plant along the sides.

2. Add a Liner

Brooke suggests burlap to hold in soil. Plastic containers with drainage do the trick too.

"You can also use sphagnum moss, which comes in sheets, although it can sometimes get a bit messy," says Brooke. Soak your moss in water before packing it into the basket, she suggests. Another option is Supamoss, made of recycled cotton fibers attached to thin plastic with small holes to let water drain. For larger baskets, you can overlap two rectangular liners, which slow the water seeping out of the basket while keeping soil from washing out. Good drainage is key to preventing root rot and keeping plants healthy.

COURTESY OF PROVEN WINNERS - WWW.PROVENWINNERS.COM

Petunias produce the best blooms when grown in full sun.

3. Select the Soil

Never fill hanging baskets with soil from your garden, warns Brooke.

"It's heavy and you risk potentially bringing pests or a disease into your hanging basket," she says.

Be sure to use good quality, lightweight potting soil, she advises. Leave an inch of space between the soil and the top of the container to allow room for watering. Check the label instructions on when to add slow-release fertilizer.

4. Pop in Plants

Most hanging baskets sport a thriller, a filler and a spiller: a taller plant in the middle such as a geranium, clumps of plants such as coleus and marigolds, and trailing plants such as petunias.

Check how big your plants will get before choosing how many to put in your basket, says Brooke. If you use too many, they won't thrive, and too few will look sparse. Also pay attention to how much light the basket will get.

She says, "I want to make sure the plants are going to survive and look great. Fuchsias are a good choice for shade and petunias or million bells can handle more sun, and they fill out baskets very well."

Add plants that come with pretty foliage, such as noninvasive dwarf ornamental grasses and ornamental sweet potatoes, she says. Give your completed basket an initial soaking, then water it regularly for gorgeous blooms all growing season.

Hummingbird Favorites

Attract hummers with flowers that grow well in hanging baskets.

- Cigar plant
- Coral bells
- Fuchsia
- Impatiens
- Lantana
- Lobelia
- Salvia
- Verbena
- Zinnia

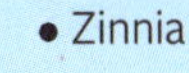

Ruby-throated hummingbird at fuchsia in a hanging basket

TOP: STEFFEN HAUSER/BOTANIKFOTO/ALAMY STOCK PHOTO; BOTTOM: ROBERT D. BARNES/GETTY IMAGES

Orange, peach and black dahlias in a vase with common hops

Grow Your Own Cutting Garden

Follow this advice for a thriving and successful plot full of perfect cut flowers

By Katy Spratte Joyce

IT'S A PRETTY PASTIME that saw a significant boost in popularity in the early days of the pandemic—and growing cut-flower gardens is poised to stay. To become a cutting-garden pro, follow the advice from a Midwest-based master. Jamie Rohda is the owner of Harvest Home Flowers in Waverly, Nebraska, a farm growing specialty cut flowers for nearly 25 years.

According to Jamie, "A cut-flower garden is a garden not meant for looks but for harvesting. Whereas a flower garden meant for the landscape is laid out for the benefit of being viewed, a cut-flower garden's purpose is to provide the owner with a continuing array of flowers to be harvested and used for floral display." That's not to say a cut-flower garden can't be aesthetically appealing; it's just not the primary intent of this type of space. To keep this goal in mind, Jamie finds that it's best, if possible, to situate a cut-flower garden where it is the least visible, so that the temptation to leave it for viewing is not as great.

Picking the Plants

Before choosing flowers, Jamie suggests that you ask yourself a series of questions to set yourself up for success:

- What amount of sun does the garden get? Will it be best to plant sun-loving flowers, or will this be a partially shaded garden?
- What are your personal likes and dislikes?
- What skills do you have? Is this your first time planting a garden, or do you already have some growing experience?
- How much growing space do you have?
- What climate zone are you in?

Jamie prefers to choose what she calls "cut and come again" blooms, which are "annual types of flowers or flowers that can be planted multiple times throughout

Iceland poppy

Zinnia

David Austin rose

Cosmos

Delphiniums

the season for the beginning grower, as they give you the most reward for your effort." Some of her go-to favorites include zinnias, ageratum, tall verbena, sunflowers, celosia, cosmos, gomphrena, dianthus and cut-flower types of marigolds. Jamie says, "With the addition of some perennials that may already be in the grower's landscape, these can provide an ongoing array of cut flowers for the entire season."

Designing the Garden

In terms of what really grows well together, the most important thing to consider is the plant size. Jamie says, "I think as long as the size is considered, almost anything works. Of course, you don't want to grow 5-foot-tall sunflowers in with 18-inch ageratum."

When designing a cut-flower bed, sunlight and water availability are the two most important things to consider. Jamie says that most easy-to-cut flowers thrive in full or nearly full sunlight, so plan accordingly. Also, if you live in an area where you need to irrigate, that should be a major consideration during the planning process. She adds one more design note in terms of functionality: "Harvesting is easiest when the garden is laid out in a nice straight bed about 3 feet across." So aim for that when creating a layout.

Maintenance Tips

Once you have everything planted, maintenance is crucial so your hard work doesn't go to waste. For lifestyle blogger, content creator and avid gardener Kate Knowles, of Kate Knowles Home, who started multiple cut-flower gardens from seed in 2021, that means visiting the garden beds almost every morning to check on things.

"Watering is my least favorite chore, so installing a drip irrigation system in our garden beds that waters everything on an automatic timer has made that chore so much easier," Kate says. "I found a video on YouTube from Garden Answer that shows the exact parts you need and instructions on installing it yourself. It wasn't too hard to figure out, and our garden benefits from consistent watering." Kate enjoys

Dahlia

Marigolds

PREVIOUS SPREAD, LEFT: GAP PHOTOS/JULIETTE WADE; BELOW, FROM LEFT: BALL HORTICULTURAL COMPANY (2); HOWARD RICE/DAVID AUSTIN ROSES; THIS SPREAD, LEFT PAGE: BALL HORTICULTURAL COMPANY (4);

Sunflower

Breadseed poppy

maintaining her three cut-flower beds (one dedicated to David Austin roses) with her three sons as a fun family activity.

How to Harvest

Finally, proper harvesting is essential when working on any cut-flower garden. Jamie suggests planning your flower harvest based on temperature: "In the cool of the morning or evening is the first place to start." Be sure to have the proper tools. "A very sharp knife is the best way to harvest cut flowers, but if you're uncomfortable with that, then a good pair of sharp snips will work," she says. "Those with a bypass-type blade (not an anvil type) will give you a good clean cut that allows the flower to drink when put in water." Cut at an angle while harvesting or arranging, Jamie says, as this will expose the most surface area so the stem can draw up water.

Kate adds that she likes to keep the seed packets for each flower in her cut garden available, as many contain harvesting instructions for optimal vase life. "Each flower has its own harvesting instructions, and usually it's best to do it in the mornings when it's not as hot outside," she says.

And the best part of a cutting-flower garden? The fresh blooms, of course. The options for using fresh flowers are limitless, but Jamie shares a few favorites: "I personally love just a few stems on my kitchen windowsill to enjoy or a collection of vases with one variety in each vase. Of course, a big mixed bouquet is always great for the dining room table! And having fresh flowers to give to a friend is always delightful for both the giver and the receiver."

Best Blooms for Cutting Gardens

- Breadseed poppies
- Cosmos
- Dahlias
- David Austin English roses
- Delphiniums
- Marigolds
- Iceland poppies
- Shirley poppies
- Sunflowers
- Sweet peas
- Zinnias

Sweet pea

Shirley poppy

RIGHT PAGE, TOP LEFT: STEPHANIE POGACHAR; TOP RIGHT: PHOTO 255895411 © PAVLAZI | DREAMSTIME.COM; BOTTOM LEFT: BALL HORTICULTURAL COMPANY; BOTTOM RIGHT: CHRISTIE KEEFER

Blooms by the Numbers

There's more to these floral families than can be seen in the backyard

Blue flag iris

Bearded iris

300

Almost 300 species exist within the iris family. Most are perennials that grow via rhizomes, which are horizontal underground plant stems that form shoots.

4 Siberian irises can reach a whopping 4 feet tall, while dwarf irises max out at 6 inches.

49 Bearded irises grow in Zones 3 to 9, which means they're found in 49 states—all except Hawaii.

6+ Most irises thrive in full sun for at least six hours per day. The rhizomes should be partially exposed to light and air to keep them dry and safe from rot.

28 You can find 28 native species of irises in the U.S., including western blue flag, crested and Klamath.

6 Bearded irises are among the most commonly planted types of irises and are divided into six different classes by the American Iris Society.

By Kaitlin Stainbrook

FROM LEFT: PHOTOSHOPPED, MARA LEE/GETTY IMAGES (2)

1753 **In 1753, a Swedish botanist mistakenly identified a flower from South Africa as part of the *Geranium* genus. Now reclassified as *Pelargonium*, that flower is still referred to as a geranium as its common name.**

280 All 300 species of cranesbill geraniums are perennial, so they'll come back each year. Plus, you can choose from roughly 280 species of *Pelargonium* geraniums, which are usually grown as annuals.

19 Charles Dickens, the well-known 19th-century author, loved scarlet pelargoniums so much that he often wore one on his jacket.

65 Overwinter pelargoniums in a sunny spot indoors if you keep your house between 60 and 65 degrees.

30 Before scents were made in laboratories, perfume companies used oils made from geranium leaves. At least 30 *Pelargonium* species are aromatic, with scents such as rose, citrus and mint.

Johnson's Blue

4-8 True geraniums, called cranesbill geraniums, form mounds of cup-shaped flowers. For a cool periwinkle color, try Johnson's Blue, hardy in Zones 4 to 8.

By Kaitlin Stainbrook

Boldly Hot Pink geranium

FROM TOP: LOPATIN ANTON/SHUTTERSTOCK; COURTESY OF PROVEN WINNERS - WWW.PROVENWINNERS.COM

300,000 **Alaskan farmers harvest about 300,000 peonies a year. Why the demand? The growing season ends in the Lower 48 by late June, but peonies thrive in July and August in Alaska.**

3-8 Herbaceous peonies do best in hardiness Zones 3 to 8 because the winters are cold enough that they encourage buds to form.

6 Peony flowers come in six forms: single, Japanese, anemone, semi-double, bomb and full double.

1,400 Peonies have been the "king of flowers" in China since the Tang dynasty (618–907 C.E.—about 1,400 years ago!) and were grown at the imperial court for their dramatic blooms.

7 Snip peonies for your favorite vase when buds are stale-marshmallow soft. A cut peony can last up to seven days.

2 California peony (*P. californica*) and Brown's peony (*P. brownii*) are the only two peony species native to North America.

33 There are 33 recognized species of peonies and 15 additional subspecies.

By Kaitlin Stainbrook

Lotus Queen peony

TONYBAGGETT/GETTY IMAGES

Show off forsythia

1804 **Originally called *Syringa suspensa*, the first identified forsythia species was renamed after Scottish botanist William Forsyth in 1804.**

10 Ready to make a statement? Meadowlark forsythia can reach up to 10 feet high if unpruned.

4 All varieties of forsythia share the same characteristic four-petaled flowers.

2 Like lilacs and crabapples, forsythia branches will flower early in a vase indoors—for an average of about two weeks—if cut while budding.

-5 Forsythia flower buds begin to drop if temperatures hit minus 5 degrees. Look for "flower-bud hardy" types for the most reliable flowering in colder areas.

11 There are about 11 species in the *Forsythia* genus, which falls under the olive family, or Oleaceae. They all hail from Asia except for one from Europe.

By Erica Browne Grivas

Made for Shade

Low-light spaces call for bright-idea plants with perks

By Deb Wiley

SHADE GARDENS OFFER MANY ADVANTAGES. Birds and pollinators need them for food, nesting and shelter. Even gardeners benefit from cooler shaded areas. But finding plants that bring color, interest and activity to your shady spaces isn't always easy.

When you want to liven up low-light areas, consider plants known for bold foliage. Invite different leaf colors and textures to mingle, such as frilly fern fronds and the lily pad-like leaves of ligularia plants. And don't forget about blooms! Plenty of colorful bloomers thrive in partial shade. Cool or light colors such as whites, pinks and blues pop in even the darkest corners of the garden.

Finally, bring a buzz of pollinator activity. Plants native to your region should always be your first choice. Here are some plant picks to get you started.

A lush shade garden full of hostas, coral bells, ferns and Japanese forest grass

Fanciful Foliage

Leaves bring as much beauty to a shade garden as blooms. Available in an array of sizes, shapes and colors, plants with unique foliage add visual interest and diversity. Grow them in multiples for big impact.

^ Lungwort

PULMONARIA, ZONES 3 TO 8

This low-growing beauty boasts fuzzy spotted or striped leaves that rest below spring blooms in hues of blue, purple, pink, red or white. Morning sun and afternoon shade keep them looking fresh.

^ Barrenwort

EPIMEDIUM, ZONES 4 TO 8

Dainty flowers in pink, purple, yellow or white appear in spring, but this plant's main draw is its durable heart-shaped leaves. They make a trouble-free ground cover, tolerating both dry and moist shade.

^ Japanese painted fern

ANISOCAMPIUM NIPONICUM, ZONES 2 TO 9

For sophisticated texture and color, consider this woodland favorite. One of the showiest cultivars is Pictum, with silvery gray fronds and burgundy red stems. For a touch of flair, try Crested Surf, which sports two frilly tips on every frond.

› Sun King Japanese spikenard

ARALIA CORDATA, ZONES 3 TO 9

With large chartreuse leaves that thrive in partial shade, this plant reaches 3 to 6 feet tall and width. A deer-resistant stunner that lives up to its regal name, it was the Perennial Plant Association's 2020 Plant of the Year.

PREVIOUS SPREAD: DOREEN WYNJA; THIS SPREAD: JAPANESE PAINTED FERN, CORAL BELLS: TERRA NOVA NURSERIES (2)

Colorful Characters

Some plants flower well in shade, especially when given morning sun. These specimens' showy blooms set the shade garden ablaze in color. But they have a lot more going for them too—attractive foliage, interesting forms and more.

^ Coral bells

HEUCHERA, ZONES 3 TO 9

Available in a wide range of leaf colors, such as amber, bronze, green, gold, pink and purple, these powerhouse plants are shade garden all-stars. Plus, the tiny flowers held aloft on wiry stems make good cut flowers.

^ Bee balm

MONARDA, ZONES 3 TO 8

This classic beauty produces more flowers in sun but can flourish when in shade, especially in hot climates. Most regions have a native or hardy species with pink, purple or red blooms that catch the eye with their spiky form.

^ Bellflower

CAMPANULA, ZONES 3 TO 9

This plant family offers blooms in many shapes and sizes, though most come in hues of pink, blue and violet. A perfect option for partial shade is Serbian bellflower, a low-growing ground cover with starry bluish purple flowers.

‹ Brunnera

BRUNNERA MACROPHYLLA, ZONES 3 TO 8

Its heart-shaped leaves with a silvery sheen and contrasting veins are unpalatable to deer. Sporting blue or white flowers in spring, the foliage of newer cultivars such as Silver Heart, Sea Heart or Jack Frost shine throughout the growing season.

LUNGWORT, SUN KING JAPANESE SPIKENARD: COURTESY OF PROVEN WINNERS - WWW.PROVENWINNERS.COM (2); BEE BALM, BELLFLOWER: WALTERS GARDENS, INC

Hummingbird Happiness

Many hummingbird-preferred flowers grow best in sun, but some do offer blooms bearing rich nectar in shade. Bees, butterflies and other pollinators will also find and appreciate them.

^ Indian pink

SPIGELIA MARILANDICA, ZONES 5 TO 9

This 1- to-2-foot-tall native deserves a place in more shade gardens. The drought tolerant, clump-forming plants produce trumpet-shaped red and yellow flowers that hummers flock to. Extend the bloom time by deadheading.

^ Hosta

HOSTA, ZONES 3 TO 9

Mainly grown for its impressive foliage, this shade-garden favorite has flowers in hues from white to lavender that attract nectar lovers. To create a hummingbird buffet, plant fragrant varieties near red-blooming plants.

^ Columbine

AQUILEGIA, ZONES 3 TO 9

Native species bloom in an array of colors, including red, yellow, orange, blue and purple. The bell-shaped flowers are nectar powerhouses. These 2- to 3-foot-tall perennials self-sow and prefer soil that drains quite quickly.

› Cardinal flower

LOBELIA CARDINALIS, ZONES 3 TO 9

With bright red or pink tubular blooms, this native does well in sun or part shade, provided it gets plenty of water. After its vibrant flowers fade, enjoy the fresh foliage and possibly a second bloom if you cut back the old spikes.

Ruby-throated hummingbird

BRUNNERA, HOSTA, GERANIUM, LIGULARIA: WALTERS GARDENS, INC (4); COLUMBINE: LINDAJOHEILMAN/GETTY IMAGES; INDIAN PINK: SEAN LEMA/SHUTTERSTOCK;

Best for Butterflies

Butterflies float toward many of the same plants beloved by other insects and hummingbirds, but they especially appreciate a shady landing pad where they can comfortably sip nectar.

^ White wood aster

EURYBIA DIVARICATA, ZONES 3 TO 8

Drought tolerant and easy to grow, this native blooms late in the season, providing butterflies with last-minute energy boosts. Tolerant of heavy shade, it grows 1 to 2 feet tall with a plethora of daisylike flowers.

^ Geranium

GERANIUM, ZONES 3 TO 8

Native geraniums, such as wild geranium, fit a wide range of growing conditions. Five-petaled blossoms in shades of pink, blue or purple grow on mounded foliage and are easy for butterflies to find and enjoy.

^ Ligularia

LIGULARIA DENTATA, ZONES 4 TO 9

These perennials boast an assortment of leaf shapes and sizes. If it's butterflies you're after, try Britt Marie Crawford with golden, daisylike flowers or Bottle Rocket with gold spires of blooms. Plant in moist soil.

‹ Turtlehead

CHELONE LYONII, ZONES 3 TO 8

Named for its flowers' resemblance to open-mouthed turtles, this late-summer bloomer attracts winged visitors with its pink, purple or white blooms. A perfect pick for rain gardens or naturalized areas, it's also deer resistant.

What Are Your Go-To Plants for Shady Spots?

Discover which flowers readers rely on to bring beauty to shadowy garden areas

With its beautiful elongated silver-speckled leaves and clumps of flowers that range from pink to red to violet, lungwort brings the first burst of spring color to my Colorado mountain flower garden. It's deer resistant and drought tolerant.

Kim Moultney TRINIDAD, CO

The large white daisylike flowers of bloodroot make me smile.

Doris Petruska TRENTON, NJ

I love bright, vivid, multicolored impatiens. In Kansas, our summers get very hot and humid, and these flowers grow well with little care.

Jennifer Broadstreet Hess MARION, KS

Soprano Salmon bedding impatiens

I use the three H's: hellebores, heucheras and hostas.

Cecilia Strakna HALETHORPE, MD

Everyone likes hostas for shady spots, but I love astilbe. Its colors and leaf shapes add a unique touch among the hostas.

Mary Ann Richter KIEL, WI

My favorite flowers for shady areas are columbines. They come in so many lovely colors!

Faith Welch JOHNSTON, RI

Heucheras, also known as coral bells

COURTESY OF PROVEN WINNERS - WWW.PROVENWINNERS.COM (2)

Dig into History

Learn about when victory gardens sprouted up across the nation

By Kaitlin Stainbrook

1917 As head of the U.S. National War Garden Commission, businessman Charles Lathrop Pack heavily promoted "war gardens" in 1917 and later helped coin the name that stuck: victory gardens.

20 By 1943, 20 million victory gardens were growing in the U.S.

40 Wartime gardeners in 1943 produced 10 billion pounds and provided 40% of the country's fresh produce supply by 1944.

1 Although most people associate victory gardens with World War II, they were first created and promoted during World War I.

11 Diana Hopkins, the 11-year-old daughter of one of President Franklin Delano Roosevelt's advisers, tended a small victory garden on the White House South Lawn.

1,000,000

More than 1 million children enrolled in the United States School Garden Army, a victory garden program for kids, in 1919.

Easy as One, Two, Tree!

Seven things to do before adding a new sapling to your property

By Rachel Maidl

Leyland cypress tree

FROM LEFT: KIYYAH, MARINA DENISENKO/GETTY IMAGES (2)

Sweetgum trees grow quickly and birds like their fruit, but the pods can be annoying to pick up. If the pros outweigh the maintenance, set aside time each fall for cleanup.

1. Assess Your Space

While the saplings in the nursery may look small, one day they could easily dwarf your home, depending on the species. Take a look around to make sure there's plenty of room for the branches to stretch outward. While you're outside, look up. Check for any overhead utility lines that the tree could touch as it grows taller. Keep in mind that trees are not one-size-fits-all. Each tree species has different spacing requirements—and many dwarf varieties can suit smaller spaces.

2. Do a Safety Check

Always call 811 three business days before digging. The service calls local utility companies to mark the location of the wires and pipes that are buried underground. This will keep you safe, ensure that your backyard project won't disrupt utility service, and help avoid costly repair bills.

3. Know the Levels

It takes time, effort and funds to nurture a new tree, so it's important to make sure it will thrive in your soil. Contact your nearest extension office and ask about its soil testing program to learn about the nutrients and acidity in your yard.

4. Pick a Tree

Here comes the fun part: picking out your tree. Consider what's important and make a list. You may want a tree that produces berries for birds, is disease resistant, offers beautiful spring flowers, has gorgeous fall color or is evergreen. Think about your climate and environment too. A tree won't survive unless it's in the right growing conditions. Start your research with these traits in mind.

5. Learn to Plant

To many new gardeners' surprise, trees require a lot of attention when they're first planted. Roots need to be kept moist—water deeply and often enough to accomplish that goal. Weather conditions and soil type influence watering frequency. Monitor the level of soil moisture daily and water as needed. Be sure to check if your water hose reaches the tree. If not, you'll be carrying many buckets of water!

6. Select Right Timing

Depending on where you live, autumn and spring are usually the best seasons to plant. Trees need time to establish themselves before dealing with hot summer sun or freezing winter ground. Once you have a tree in mind, look up what planting season suits it best.

7. Plan for Upkeep

Some trees require more cleanup and tidying than others. For instance, the branches of weeping willow trees need to be trimmed to stay off the ground, and sweetgum pods may need to be raked up. Set aside time for this annual plant maintenance—then sit back and watch your new tree grow.

Best for Birds

Seven trees that provide shelter or food for fliers.

- American redbud
- Apple serviceberry
- Flowering dogwood
- Hackberry
- Leyland cypress
- Snowdrift crabapple
- Southern magnolia

Blooms for Birds

Attract goldfinches, cardinals and other eager seed eaters from summer through winter with a selection of annuals

By Sally Roth

Perched on Petals

Zinnias are attractive to various seed-eating songbirds, but ruby-throated hummingbirds also stop by for nectar.

FOR A BIG SPLASH OF COLOR THAT LASTS FOR MONTHS, YOU CAN'T BEAT ANNUAL FLOWERS. But beauty is only the beginning. Once the blooms of graceful cosmos, cheerful sunflowers, dramatic dark-leaved amaranths, bold zinnias and other easy-to-grow annuals start to fade, the real fun begins. That's when they bring in the birds!

Even the best feeder foods often take a backseat to flower seeds. And watching a flock of goldfinches forage naturally among your plants is even more entertaining than seeing them on a tube feeder. That's true for the dozens of bird species that avidly eat the seeds of annuals, whether it's northern cardinals snapping up gomphrena, towhees carefully taking tithonia, or native sparrows and juncos energetically scratching beneath the marigolds.

Backyard Entertainment

Wildlife biologist Terry W. Johnson of Georgia marvels at the appeal. "When you see how small some of these seeds are, and how hard the cardinals work to get the tiny seeds when right nearby are black oil sunflower seeds at the feeder, it's amazing!" he says.

Annuals typically begin to attract songbirds in late summer, when the first flowers start to produce seeds. "If zinnias are blooming on your deck or in your garden, keep your eyes peeled for petals scattered beneath the plants," Terry urges. It's a clue that goldfinches have been enjoying a late summer banquet, even before the seeds fully ripen. Terry sees the same telltale sign of bird activity beneath his containers of scarlet sage, a native wildflower that he has discovered is a favorite of northern cardinals.

Watch Closely

Seed eaters are surprisingly tricky to spot among flowers and foliage. Watch for motion—of both birds and plants. Willowy cosmos stems sway under the weight of goldfinches; marigolds and ornamental millet will bend to the ground as juncos and sparrows jump up to pull down seed heads; flashes of wings will give away cardinals, jays, chickadees and others sampling the sunflowers.

"While I was drinking my coffee and gazing out the window over the kitchen sink, I saw the globe amaranth plants in one of our deck containers

Cosmos

Mourning doves temporarily store seeds in their crop—a pocket in their throat.

LEFT: LAURA PETTIGREW; RIGHT, TOP: DOREENWYNJA.COM PHOTOGRAPHY; RIGHT, BOTTOM: BOB KOTHENBEUTEL

Rose-breasted grosbeaks, such as this one in a crabapple, have strong beaks for eating seeds.

violently shaking," Terry says. "A female cardinal had landed on them and was pulling apart their flower heads! After tearing apart several blossoms to reach the tiny seeds hidden inside, the bird snipped off an entire flower head and flew away."

Because annuals put out new blossoms, and lots of them, the bird banquet lasts for months, long after the plants are hit by a killing frost. For gardeners who may be tempted to pull out the dead plants, "simply resist the impulse to create a tidy garden," Terry says. "Let the plants remain standing if you want to add a new facet to bird feeding. You will be providing a great source of food, and you'll enjoy watching fascinating bird behavior."

Easy Bird Buffets

Scatter annual seeds in a sunny spot and lightly cover them for blooms in as little as six weeks, or buy started plants. The most likely diners are goldfinches, native sparrows, juncos, towhees, northern cardinals and doves. Surprises such as grosbeaks, crossbills, buntings, redpolls or pine siskins may show up too.

Annuals for Every Space

Even a small bed of flowers will bring in the birds. So will container gardens, which Terry and his wife especially enjoy. "As we get older, our eyesight is not as good as it used to be," he says. "Containers bring wildlife closer to the window. We don't even have to go outside."

A bigger annual garden will attract more birds, and more kinds of birds. Not only does it offer more seeds, but it also provides the sheltering cover that makes birds feel at home. Plant annuals around your birdbath, feeder area, garden gnome or other outdoor ornaments, and add containers of them to your garden beds. Human-made objects create a sense of orderliness, even in winter. The flower show may be finished, but songbirds add a whole second act!

Try a variety of bird-favored annuals, but grow some of them in dense patches or rows of the same kind, instead of dotting them around. A concentrated swath of color looks great in bloom—and when seeds ripen, the patch provides the cover that songbirds seek. Be sure to plant some of your annuals a few feet from a favorite window or near an outdoor sitting area, so you can watch birds seek out the seeds as long as they last.

Indigo bunting on sunflower

FROM LEFT: JOHN GILL; STEVE AND DAVE MASLOWSKI; RICHARD DAY/DAYBREAK IMAGERY

CHAPTER 2

Summer

Get your garden summer-ready with water-wise picks and drought-resistant plants that roll out the green carpet for birds and bees. Sustainable never looked so lush!

Easy Breezy Gardening

Seven tips for a beautiful low-maintenance yard with minimal fuss and effort

Lilacs

NANCY HATTEN

1. Water Less Frequently

Choose drought-tolerant plants, trees and shrubs that require less water to thrive. It makes sense to reduce the number of times you need to lug a full watering can or hose around the yard, plus watering restrictions are a reality in many areas. Plenty of beautiful native options work in a variety of climates and soils with little water.

The keys are to carefully match the plant to its new growing conditions and to water it consistently until it's established. Once it has a good root system, it will grow with minimal supplemental water.

2. Let Go of Lawn Care

Many folks love their grass lawns but, frankly, an attractive lawn can require lots of upkeep. Replace a patch of grass with an appropriate ground cover plant to slash your chore time without sacrificing a lush, lovely yard.

Swap turf in problem spots such as shady, hot or rocky areas with a ground cover that grows in those conditions. Check with your local university extension service for a list of plants suited for your area.

3. Pick Healthy Options

Many new trees and shrubs are bred to resist disease and pests. They tend to be healthier and more self-sufficient and need fewer treatments. Plus, they're more likely to last, which decreases the odds that you'll need to dig one up and replace it in the future.

4. Go Small

Plant breeders are also developing smaller plants. This means garden favorites can fit into small spaces without extensive pruning. Dwarf Globe blue spruce, upright Skyrocket juniper, and smaller ninebarks, such as Summer Wine or Little Devil, all have fantastic qualities and require minimal pruning to fit into tinier spaces.

5. Add Living Space

Patio pavers set in a grid and surrounded by landscaping rocks make an elegant, simple and environmentally friendly surface for an outdoor lounge set. Walkways, patios, courtyards and other elements add a bit of magic to any yard while also reducing landscaping chores.

Choose materials and designs that allow rain to permeate the soil, irrigate surrounding plantings, minimize erosion and prevent runoff. These include gravel, organic mulches, crushed stone and permeable pavers.

Coneflowers

6. Make Room for Mulch

Weed less by mulching. Apply a layer of wood chips or bark at least a few inches thick every two or three years. That way, the soil will also retain moisture more readily, meaning you can water less.

Avoid turning the soil, as it may likely expose dormant weed seeds to moisture and air, causing them to sprout. Instead, let the earthworms from your compost or healthy soil do the cultivating for you.

7. Skip Fussy Flowers

Gardeners love roses, but most need a bounty of water, fertilizer and attention to look their best. You shouldn't give up everything you love, but choose your plantings carefully. If the majority of your landscape is relatively carefree, you'll have more time to keep your finicky plants happy.

THOMAS JONES

A Summer Staple

Besides it being a pollinator magnet, there are countless reasons to add colorful salvia to your yard

By Kelsey Roseth

TO BIRDERS, THERE ARE ENDLESS REASONS to love salvia—this spectacular plant does a lot of good.

"It is easy to grow, a prolific bloomer that comes in a variety of colors and is very versatile," says Wendy Wilber, the Florida statewide master gardener volunteer coordinator for the University of Florida, IFAS Extension Service.

Female ruby-throated hummingbird

LEFT: ROBYNMAC; THIS IMAGE: MICHAEL LEE/GETTY IMAGES (2)

Bee on salvia

TOP LEFT: JANE THIRSK/GETTY IMAGES

Meant to Be Manageable

This member of the mint family (*Lamiaceae*) is low maintenance and resistant to deer and disease, in addition to being a great garden pick to attract pollinators. There are hundreds of annual and perennial species of salvia available worldwide.

Adds Flavor to Food

Salvia also has an aromatic allure. "You take that leaf and scrunch it up in your hand, and it smells awesome," says Luke Nygaard, owner of Nygaard Nursery in Dilworth, Minnesota.

A variety of this plant produces the sage used in seasonings, while others have flowers that provide an attractive garnish for dishes including salads, butters and soft cheeses.

History of Natural Medicine

Salvia comes from the Latin word *salvere,* which means "to heal." According to *The Old Farmer's Almanac,* "Ancient Romans believed that salvia stimulated the brain and memory; they also used it to clean their teeth." The National Library of Medicine recognizes salvia as a traditional medicine that was used to reduce pain and inflammation, and to protect against oxidative stress and free radical damage.

Finding a New Favorite

Salvia's bright blooms are visible through midsummer and fall—whenever it gets hot in your zone. Amid velvet leaves, the flowers come in plenty of colors, from purples and pinks to blues, reds and whites.

Salvia's incredible colors play a large part in each cultivar's appeal. "May Night is a perennial salvia that is drop-dead gorgeous. Absolutely beautiful," Luke says of its bright purple spikes.

"My favorite, which is Wendy's Wish, is a hot pink," says Wendy, who appreciates that a portion of each sale of a Wendy's Wish salvia benefits Make-A-Wish Australia.

Ask your local garden center about new cultivars. "Proven Winners is doing a lot of work on these. They have a series called Rockin',"

Pink Profusion

Wendy says. Rockin' Deep Purple blooms a bold, royal purple. Rockin' Fuchsia is a new cultivar featuring a flush of alluring pink.

If you are looking for nectar and seed production for pollinators, Wendy encourages searching for native options, as they will be the best at attracting the wildlife in your zone.

Creating Ideal Conditions

Most salvias thrive in bright, full sun and require good drainage.

Make sure to provide enough room for growth. These plants range from 1 to 6 feet tall and wide, though most average 2 to 3 feet.

Salvias can be planted in the spring or fall in a variety of soils. "They're jolly either way," Luke says.

Organic mulch benefits these plants by protecting their roots, helping maintain a suitable soil temperature and keeping moisture consistent. For those with heavy or clay soil, plant "proud," meaning the plant should sit slightly higher than the surrounding ground.

TOP AND RIGHT: COURTESY OF PROVEN WINNERS - WWW.PROVENWINNERS.COM (2)

Wendy's Wish

May Night

Color Spires Snow Kiss

Dare to Deadhead

Salvias create dramatic displays in cottage gardens—and they're a great option if you want to soften borders and pathways. They also spill beautifully from containers. To continue encouraging blooms, prune this plant.

"As soon as those blooms are spent, instead of going just below the flower spike, I go one more node down to stimulate new growth to come out of the sides of the stems," says Wendy, who does this to boost the chance of two new stems.

Benefit Pollinators

Salvias rely on bees, butterflies and birds. And hummingbirds are drawn to this nectar-packed plant's colorful spikes of tubular flowers.

To further support visiting pollinators, place a water source nearby, offer open soil for ground burrowers and provide shelter through a small brush pile. You can also install bee boxes.

Success with Seeds

If you are new to salvia and are starting plants from seed, make sure conditions are consistent and aligned with recommendations. Start them six to eight weeks before your zone's final frost.

When bringing them outside, "Do a good job of hardening them off, which means preparing them for their life outdoors, or you may get frustrated," says Luke, whose nursery is in Zone 4. "You've got to give them tough love."

Rockin Fuchsia

WENDY'S WISH: ARLIFTATOZ2205/SHUTTERSTOCK; MAY NIGHT: WALTERS GARDENS, INC; SNOW KISS, ROCKIN' FUCHSIA: COURTESY OF PROVEN WINNERS - WWW.PROVENWINNERS.COM (2)

SPLINE_X/SHUTTERSTOCK

Advice for Arrangements

Salvia's slender blooms contribute to long-lasting, beautiful bouquets when you:

- identify one of a salvia's main stems.
- cut 1 inch above the stem's bottom.
- slice the stem at a 45-degree angle.
- arrange in your favorite vase.
- remove submerged foliage.

This process also encourages another batch of blooms on the plant where it is cut.

Incredible Edible Shrubs

Plant picks that look good in a landscape and provide a tasty treat for you and backyard wildlife

By Niki Jabbour

Highbush blueberries

FROM LEFT: TOMASZ PAWLUS, DIANA TALIUN/SHUTTERSTOCK (2)

Blue grosbeak on elderberry bush

Gooseberries

THESE WOODY, MULTISTEMMED PLANTS ADD YEAR-ROUND INTEREST, provide shelter to wildlife and create privacy. And when you select the ones that also have edible fruits, flowers, leaves or nuts, it's as if you've won the botanical lottery.

Horticulturist and author Steven Biggs of *Food Garden Life* grows a wide variety of edible shrubs such as currants, gooseberries, medlars and elderberries in his Toronto garden. "My edible shrubs," he says, "offer bird habitat as well as nectar-rich blossoms for pollinators and reliable annual harvests to eat—or, in the case of elderflower champagne, drink."

Shrub Considerations

Success begins with picking edible species that are best suited for your region. Research or read plant labels to check the shrub's hardiness zone range. It's also important to look at the area where you plan to grow it to see how much direct sunlight it'll receive. Certain shrubs, such as highbush blueberries, grow and produce best in full sun, while others, such as currants, can get away with less light.

Extra Benefits

If you're looking for a privacy hedge, consider shrub roses, which can grow to a variety of heights—some reach up to 7 or 8 feet tall—while offering hips that are high in vitamin C. Another option is sea-buckthorn, a dense-growing shrub with bright orange berries and thorns that keep out unwanted visitors. Low-growing edible shrubs, such as currants, are perfect for creating bed borders or garden edgings.

Birds, squirrels and other types of wildlife also love shrubs with fruits or nuts. If you're willing to share, grow extra plants so there's plenty to go around. But if you want to prevent pilfering, drape bird netting over the plants or use a fruit cage.

Red currant jam

TOP SHRUB PICKS

Pink Icing blueberries

Highbush blueberries

VACCINIUM CORYMBOSUM, ZONES 3 TO 9

Not only do highbush blueberries produce a generous crop of summer berries, but they also have dainty spring flowers that are beloved by native bees, along with bright autumn foliage. Plant in a sunny site with well-draining, acidic soil, and check to see if this or any other fruiting plants you plan to grow have winter chill requirements. Most cultivars grow 5 to 8 feet tall, and it's best to plant two different ones to guarantee pollination and a good fruit set.

Gooseberry jam

American hazelnut

American elderberry

SAMBUCUS CANADENSIS, ZONES 4 TO 9

A North American native, this deciduous shrub grows 6 to 12 feet tall. It's a great choice for a damp spot because it's tolerant of wet soils while also happy in average garden soil. It produces summer sprays of fragrant white flowers that you can pick for fritters, custards or garnishes. By late summer, the purple-black berries are ripe and ready for winemaking, syrups, jellies and pie fillings. American elderberry is self-fruiting, which means it does not require cross-pollination and can produce fruit from pollination with the pollen of its own flowers, but you'll get more berries if there are two or more plants.

Gooseberries

RIBES SPP., ZONES 3 TO 8

Gooseberries are a great option where space is tight. The shrubs grow just 3 to 5 feet tall and wide and are self-fruiting, so you only need one plant. The light green to pink fruits mature from early summer to midsummer. Grow this shrub in full sun or part shade along a foundation, in a mixed border or as a low hedge.

BLUEBERRY: BUSHEL AND BERRY; HAZELNUT: NANCY J. ONDRA, CRANBERRY: MANFRED RUCKSZIO, CHOKECHERRY: WASILISA/SHUTTERSTOCK (3); JAM: FOTOATELIE, QUINCE: VOLOSINA, HONEYBERRY:

Elderberry

American hazelnut

CORYLUS AMERICANA, ZONES 4 TO 9

This is an easy, fast-growing shrub that yields a heavy crop of protein- and nutrient-rich nuts. The plant, also known as American filbert, grows 8 to 12 feet tall and wide, and does well in full sun to part shade. You'll need at least two plants for effective cross-pollination, and they should be grown relatively close together. The nuts mature in late summer and are delicious both raw and roasted.

Currants

RIBES SPP., ZONES 3 TO 8

Compact, cold-hardy and very productive, currant shrubs produce clusters of jewel-like fruits in red, pink, black and white that are perfect to eat fresh or as jams and jellies. "It's a pity these pectin-rich fruits aren't better known, because they tolerate shade and many types of soil, making them great for edible landscapes, edible hedges, food forests and traditional backyard gardens," says Steve. While currants (and gooseberries) were once prohibited from many states because of white pine blister rust, many bans have since been repealed. But do your research before buying to make sure they're allowed where you live.

"We freeze enough currants to make loads of preserves and cordial all winter long," Steve says.

Bonus Edible Shrubs

American cranberry
VACCINIUM MACROCARPON, ZONES 2 TO 7

Chokecherry
PRUNUS VIRGINIANA, ZONES 3 TO 7

Flowering quince
CHAENOMELES SPECIOSA, ZONES 4 TO 8

Honeyberry
LONICERA CAERULEA, ZONES 2 TO 7

Jostaberry
RIBES × NIDIGROLARIA, ZONES 3 TO 7

Medlar
MESPILUS GERMANICA, ZONES 5 TO 8

Sea-buckthorn
HIPPOPHAE RHAMNOIDES, ZONES 3 TO 7

Serviceberry
AMELANCHIER SPP., ZONES 3 TO 8

Plants with Flavors

Get ready to add punch to your cocktails, teas and more

By Wendy Helfenbaum

Potted Perfection

English lavender in a container can be moved to a porch or a back patio for easy access and a boost of fragrance.

‹ English lavender

LAVANDULA ANGUSTIFOLIA, ZONES 5 TO 8

Bring in the bees and butterflies with this lovely and fragrant perennial bloomer. Plenty of sun and well-draining, slightly alkaline soil help it thrive all summer. Its sweet floral notes complement berries, pears and citrus flavors when used sparingly either in a simple syrup or as a fresh mix-in.

Add it to: Martinis, lavender-sage slings, gin sours, hot or iced tea, lemonade, or seltzer. Or infuse it into vodka.

^ Lemon verbena

ALOYSIA CITRIODORA, ZONES 8 TO 10 OR ANNUAL

With its bright citrus taste and spear-shaped leaves, this sun-loving perennial needs rich and well-draining soil. It grows to 4 feet tall, and its leaves can be harvested by cutting the entire stem. Clusters of white or purple flowers delight beneficial insects.

Add it to: Gin and tonic or gimlet cocktails. The fresh or dried leaves and the blossoms all make great iced tea too—try combining the verbena with mint and honey.

^ Common juniper

JUNIPERUS COMMUNIS, ZONES 2 TO 7

This conifer's berries are actually tiny, scale-covered blue cones. Citrusy and slightly bitter, they are used to flavor gin and some types of beer. Sun-loving common juniper grows up to 10 feet tall and 12 feet wide and features needlelike, fragrant leaves. Some junipers are poisonous, so research your plant before picking.

Add it to: Gin fizzes, gin and tonic cocktails, champagne, tea or lemonade.

‹ Siam Queen Thai basil

OCIMUM BASILICUM VAR. THYRSIFLORA, ZONES 10 TO 11

The purple stems and flowers of this plant pack a tasty punch with hints of licorice and lemon. Thai basil likes warm, moist, well-draining soil, along with six hours of direct sunlight per day. Plant fresh batches each year for maximum flavor.

Add it to: Spicy cucumber rum cocktails, gimlets, martinis, daiquiris or lemonade. Its flowers make gorgeous garnishes too.

COMMON JUNIPER: AKCHAMCZUK/GETTY IMAGES (2); SIAM QUEEN THAI BASIL: W. ATLEE BURPEE COMPANY

^ Pineapple sage

SALVIA ELEGANS, ZONES 8 TO 11

This plant produces scarlet tubular flowers, and its leaves release a sweet, tropical scent when crushed. Pineapple sage is heat and drought tolerant. It prefers full sun, and the blooms attract butterflies as well as hummingbirds.

Add it to: Rum juleps, mojitos, tequila sours or iced tea. Tuck whole fresh flowering stems into fruity drinks or lemonade. Sprinkle petals on top of a frosty pina colada or freeze them into gorgeous ice cubes.

^ Parisian Gherkin F1 cucumbers

CUCUMIS SATIVUS, ANNUAL

These mini black-spined gherkin cukes are delicious fresh or pickled. The compact, semi-vining plant thrives in sunshine and grows quickly in raised beds or staked containers. Harvest regularly when the cucumbers are 2 to 4 inches long.

Add it to: Vodka martinis, cucumber Collins, watermelon cucumber-tinis or spicy cucumber-mint margaritas. Or mix it with gin, lime and mint.

› Roselle hibiscus

HIBISCUS SABDARIFFA, ZONES 8 TO 11

Related to okra, this statement plant features crimson stems, red-veined leaves and pink flowers. It needs full sun and 12 or more hours of darkness for the most blooms. Grow it in the ground or in a pot. Its flowers and calyxes flavor beverages with a tangy, cranberrylike taste.

Add it to: Rose hip tea with dried orange peel or a squeeze of lime. Try freezing it in ice cubes to liven up cold drinks.

PINEAPPLE SAGE: COURTESY OF PROVEN WINNERS - WWW.PROVENWINNERS.COM; PARISIAN GHERKIN

^ Alpine strawberry

FRAGARIA VESCA, ZONES 5 TO 9

Also known as the wild or woodland strawberry, this compact decorative perennial can handle full sun to part shade and can be grown indoors too. It bears fruit continually throughout the growing season.

Add it to: Cordials, rosé wine, gin, strawberry-basil lemonade or a wild-strawberry fizz with rum.

^ Chocolate mint

MENTHA X PIPERITA F. CITRATA, ZONES 5 TO 9

This fast-growing plant thrives in rich, moist soil under full to part sun and grows up to 2 feet tall. Its dark green leaves smell like chocolate but have a minty orange taste. Spiky lavender blossoms appear in July and August and attract butterflies.

Add it to: Hot water to make chocolate mint tea. Or make a simple syrup for mojitos and gin sodas.

RHUBARB: BALL HORTICULTURAL COMPANY

‹ Rhubarb

RHEUM X CULTORUM, ZONES 3 TO 8

Cold-hardy and drought-tolerant rhubarb is a classic that loves full sun and rich, well-draining, loamy soil. Divide plants every four years in spring or fall for continued health and harvest.

Add it to: Mojitos or gin-based strawberry rhubarb Collins. Rhubarb simple syrup is a versatile cocktail ingredient.

Pot-a-peno pepper

Grow Minis!

The ultimate guide to small-space veggie gardening

By Carol J. Michel

IN THE LATE 1980S, I carved out space for my first vegetable garden from a 1-foot-wide strip of soil between my patio and a fence. I did my best to squeeze some green beans and a few tomato plants into that little space. Today, dozens of mini vegetable varieties are on the market, allowing me to squeeze even more into a small space.

What Are Mini Vegetables?

Mini vegetables are also referred to as dwarf or compact vegetables. According to Josh Kirschenbaum of PanAmerican Seed, no parameters are set for what defines a dwarf vegetable, but they are notably smaller than a standard-size plant and can perform well in a pot.

Like full-size vegetable plants, dwarf or mini types usually require full sun. When they're grown in containers, these plants will need more frequent watering—as often as once or twice a day during the hottest days of summer, depending on the size of the container. You'll also need to fertilize them more often because frequent watering quickly leaches out the nutrients that the vegetables need to thrive.

A History Lesson

As Jennifer McGuinness noted in her book *Micro Food Gardening: Project Plans and Plants for Growing Fruits and Veggies in Tiny Spaces,* people are moving to cities, and by 2050, well over half of us will live in an urban environment. Fortunately, the plant industry recognizes this. About 15 years ago, breeders at companies such as PanAmerican Seed started creating dwarf vegetable varieties with a focus on those that grow well in both containers and hydroponic systems such as the AeroGarden.

Why Grow Minis

You won't harvest bushels of produce when you grow mini vegetables or fruits, but it's still beneficial to grow them.

ENJOY HOMEGROWN TASTE. You'll discover that homegrown vegetables, even small ones, often taste better than varieties you buy in grocery stores. Plus you can't get fresher vegetables than those you pick and eat right away. If you grow dwarf vegetables using a simple indoor hydroponic system, you can also get that fresh taste year-round.

SPEND LESS TIME AND EFFORT. Planting mini vegetables in containers takes less time and overall effort than planting a vegetable garden in the ground.

TEACH KIDS ABOUT FOOD. When they see dwarf vegetables growing up close, they learn where their food comes from.

GAIN EXPERIENCE TO GROW FULL-SIZE VEGETABLES. You may be timid about planting a large vegetable garden, even if you have the space for it. But after success with dwarf vegetables, you may have the desire to grow regular-size plants.

The Challenges

Growing dwarf vegetables isn't completely trouble free. Small plants can still be attacked by the same insect pests and diseases found in in-ground vegetable gardens.

Besides the extra time required for watering and fertilizing, dwarf vegetable types require more investment. A hydroponic system or containers and potting soil can cost quite a bit initially. Fortunately, most containers can be reused for years.

LEFT: ALL-AMERICA SELECTIONS; RIGHT: ETIAMMOS/SHUTTERSTOCK.COM

10 MINI VEGGIE PLANTS TO TRY

1. Lizzano tomato

If you are looking for a classic cherry tomato for a container on your patio, try Lizzano.

This variety produces fruit over a long period and is resistant to late blight. In a container on the ground, it will need a cage or other support, but it also does well in a large hanging basket where it can hang down from the edges.

- Start seeds indoors six to eight weeks before your first frost-free date or buy plants in late spring.
- Harden off seedlings by placing them outside in shade for a few hours a day when temperatures are above 60.
- Plant seedlings in the container once there is no risk of frost.

1 Lizzano tomato

2. Quickfire pepper

Round out your mini veggie collection with a hot Thai-type pepper called Quickfire. An All-America Selections winner from 2022, it produces hot peppers on smaller plants and is perfect for containers. The hot peppers show above the foliage so they are easy to harvest.

Some gardeners wonder if sweet peppers turn hot when grown next to hot peppers. But they don't. Growing them near each other won't affect the taste of either one.

- Make sure you start your seeds inside six to eight weeks before your first frost-free date or buy plants in late spring.
- Harden off seedlings by placing them outside in shade for a few hours a day when temperatures are above 60.
- Once there is no risk of frost, go ahead and plant seedlings in their container.

2 Quickfire pepper

3. Cal Sweet Bush watermelon

You may think there is no way you can grow a watermelon in a container, but you can! Cal Sweet Bush is a compact bush-type plant with short vines that performs quite well in containers.

Let it grow all summer, and you'll have your own homegrown watermelon in about 90 days. Grow it in full sun and keep it watered throughout the summer.

- Sow seeds directly outside in a large container.
- Thin to one seedling—choose the strongest one—by carefully pulling out the other seedlings.

4. Emerald Towers basil

Emerald Towers is a tall basil plant that grows almost straight up, making it a good accent plant in a container with other edibles. Plus, it's slow to produce flowers, which allows you to harvest its leaves for most of the growing season. The plants don't need a large container to grow in, but they should be watered regularly.

- Start seeds indoors four to five weeks before your first frost-free date or buy plants in late spring.

1: ALL-AMERICA SELECTIONS; 2: BALL HORTICULTURAL COMPANY; 3: ALL-AMERICA SELECTIONS; 4, PEAS: W. ATLEE BURPEE COMPANY (2)

Cal Sweet Bush watermelon

Emerald Towers basil

- When temperatures are above 60, place the seedlings outside in the shade for a few hours to harden off.
- Once there is no risk of frost, plant the seedlings in their container. Or direct sow seeds in pots outdoors after your garden is frost-free.

5. Mascotte green bean

Like many beloved veggies, this one tastes best when it's freshly picked. If you are low on space but want to grow beans, try Mascotte, a dwarf type that produces beans up to 5 inches long. Its mature height is about 20 inches.

Keep picking the beans as they mature, which takes about 50 days from sowing, and the plants should keep flowering and produce more beans for several weeks.

- Sow seeds directly in containers when the possibility of frost has passed, spacing the seeds as per the instructions on the packet.
- The seeds should germinate within a few days.

6. Katarina cabbage

It's surprising how big a cabbage plant can get and how much better homegrown cabbage tastes. Try Katarina, which produces a small, tasty head of cabbage and grows well in large containers. This cabbage tolerates light frost, so you can get an early start by putting it outside a few weeks before your last frost.

Mature cabbage heads should be ready to harvest in about six weeks.

- Sow seeds indoors four to six weeks before transplanting outdoors or buy transplants in early spring.
- To keep cabbage butterfly larvae from eating the leaves, use a lightweight floating row cover.

Love Fresh Peas?

You can grow Peas-in-a-Pot on your patio too. Bred for containers and small space gardens, it's a 10-inch plant with a good yield. Check it out at *burpee.com*.

7
Patio Baby eggplant

8
Patio Choice Yellow tomato

7. Patio Baby eggplant

Even if you usually don't like eggplant, try growing this dwarf variety and cooking the small, tasty eggplants it produces. Because the plants top out at less than 2 feet tall, they do well in large containers placed in full sun.

A unique feature of this eggplant variety is that it doesn't have thorns on the leaves or the calyx (that green cap where the eggplant attaches to the plant). This is a big plus at harvest time.

- Start seeds indoors six to eight weeks before your frost-free date or purchase plants in late spring.
- Harden off the seedlings by placing them outside in shade for a few hours a day when temperatures are above 60.
- Plant seedlings in their pot once there is no risk of frost.

8. Patio Choice Yellow tomato

Cherry tomatoes may be small, but that's not true of all cherry tomato plants. Patio Choice Yellow is a smaller plant that does well on a patio in a pot.

To keep your tomatoes (and all mini vegetables in containers) healthy, fertilize them regularly with a liquid fertilizer.

- Start seeds indoors six to eight weeks before your first frost-free date or buy plants in late spring.
- Harden off seedlings by placing them outside in shade for a few hours a day when temperatures are above 60 degrees.
- Plant seedlings in their container once there is no risk of frost.

9. Pot-a-peno pepper

Pot-a-peno is a jalapeno-type pepper that grows well in a pot or a hanging basket from which it can cascade down the sides.

You can pick the peppers while green or let them ripen to red. Not only will the color change, but the flavor will too. Try them both ways!

- Start seeds indoors six to eight weeks before your first frost-free date or buy plants in late spring.
- Harden off seedlings by placing them outside in shade for a few hours a day when temperatures are above 60.
- Plant seedlings in their container once the risk of frost has passed.

10. Patio Snacker cucumber

Patio Snacker is a dwarf vegetable variety that you can grow in a large container. Cucumber plants are vines, so add a small trellis to give them something to climb up.

The big surprise is that this plant, although smaller than most

Tabletop Vegetables

If your only growing space is a sunny windowsill or a small table outdoors, "tabletop vegetables" may be your best option. Kitchen Minis from PanAmerican Seed were bred to be grown in small containers.

Several varieties of sweet peppers, hot peppers and cherry tomatoes are available now. A Quick Snack cucumber is available since 2024. Find out more at *kitchenminis.com*.

7, 8, 10: ALL-AMERICA SELECTIONS (3); TABLETOP CUCUMBER: BALL HORTICULTURAL COMPANY

Patio Snacker cucumber

cucumber plants, produces larger cucumbers, up to 7 to 8 inches long, in 50 days or so.

Keep picking the cucumbers to encourage the vine to keep flowering. Most cucumber plants produce separate male and female flowers and need bees to pollinate them, but Patio Snacker does not need insect pollination.

- Sow seeds directly outside in a large container.
- Thin to one or two seedlings by carefully pulling out the other seedlings or by cutting off the extra seedlings at soil level.

Quick Tips for Choosing Mini Vegetables

Choose vegetables you already love to eat. Maybe try one or two you don't typically prefer and see if you like the homegrown version.

Check the plant's mature size. *Dwarf, mini, compact* and *ultra compact* are all terms used to describe smaller veggie plants. Read the label to determine the mature size so you won't be surprised.

Find out how big the veggies will be at harvest time. Some dwarf plants produce much smaller vegetables, while others grow vegetables that are almost full size.

Don't limit yourself to just vegetable plants labeled as dwarf, compact, mini, etc. Also look for full-size varieties—which may actually be naturally smaller plants to begin with—that are described as growing well in containers.

Finally, choose a few varieties that you can eat as you pick them. Nothing is better than a fresh, sun-warmed cherry tomato right off the vine.

Oops! Common Tomato Mistakes

Vine-ripe tomatoes are some of summer's great joys—here's how to avoid 11 missteps and harvest a bumper crop

By Lisa Kaminski

1. Forgetting There Are Different Tomato Types

Perhaps the greatest decision to make with your tomato garden is whether you want to plant determinate or indeterminate plants.

Determinate tomatoes grow to a particular height and produce all their fruit in a short time span—within a month or two—in the summer. They work well for folks who want to harvest many tomatoes at once for projects such as making and preserving tomato sauce.

Indeterminate plants will continue to grow and produce fruit until frost hits or you pinch off the growing tips. These are great if you want to have access to fresh tomatoes throughout the warm months.

2. Thinking All Heirloom Tomatoes Are the Same

The word *heirloom* conjures images of gorgeous but irregular tomatoes in all sorts of hues. Remember: Not all heirloom tomatoes are the same. It's a catchall term for varieties over 50 years old that haven't changed over time. They offer different shapes, colors and flavors. Do a little research to find out what makes a particular heirloom variety special.

Dragon's Eye tomato

3. Planting Earlier Than Recommended

Tomato plants like it warm, so gardeners in the north shouldn't rush to put plants in the ground the second the snow melts. Instead, wait until freezing temperatures are long past. Tomato plants won't survive a frost without cover, so be sure that the nights don't get too cold and that the days are warm and sunny to help your tomatoes grow. Read the instructions on seed packets and plant tags to know when to start the growing season.

4. Growing Too Close Together

You may think that more plants means more tomatoes. But this isn't always true. Crowding your plants limits the sun and airflow the leaves get. If plants don't get all the fresh air and sunlight they need, they'll yield less fruit or possibly develop diseases.

Give tomato plants ample room to grow—about 3 feet between each plant is best, depending on the variety.

5. Using Small Pots

When it comes to planting tomatoes in containers, remember that bigger is better. You want to give them plenty of nutrient-rich soil and enough room to put down roots. Also, larger pots hold moisture longer than small ones, so you won't have to water as frequently.

6. Fertilizing at the Wrong Time

Fertilizers do wonders to boost the growth of plants. A soil test will tell you what type and how much to add. For months of benefits, try a slow-release fertilizer at planting. Be sure to avoid high-nitrogen fast-release fertilizers when tomatoes are in

Yellow Pear heirloom cherry tomatoes

their prime, as they promote leaf and stem growth—not flower and fruit production. And remember to always follow instructions on the fertilizer label.

7. Placing in the Shade

Tomato plants require full sun—a shady spot just won't work. If sun is at a premium in your yard, give your tomatoes the best spot. Other veggies (such as beets, carrots, kale and other greens) can handle a bit of shade.

Green Zebra heirloom

8. Staking After They're Unruly

Growing more like vines than shrubs, tomatoes need the support of stakes or cages. But don't wait till they've grown large and leggy. The best time to give tomatoes support is before they really need it. Plus, smaller plants are easier to adjust so there's no fighting your way through all those leaves. Be sure to use a support system that's large enough for the variety you are growing.

9. Skipping Companion Plants

While companion plants aren't necessary, they can be advantageous. Certain plants improve the soil and others shelter helpful insects that eat garden pests.

10. Passing on Pruning

Tomato plants tend to get a little leggy over time—and that's fine! Just remember to prune them strategically. Early in the season, trim away small stems, sometimes called suckers, along the base and stem of the plant. This will focus the plant's energy on creating a strong stem.

About a month before the end of the growing season, snip off the very top of the tomato plant. This encourages the plant to ripen the last fruits instead of growing taller.

11. Picking the Same Spot Every Year

Changing location helps reduce the risk of insects and disease. Plus, all plants draw nutrients from the soil, and tomatoes in particular soak up a lot. If space allows, switch up where you grow your plants. Or make sure that you replenish the soil with compost and fertilizer to support your plants.

Time to Pick!

While tomatoes are best vine-ripened, it could be a mistake to wait for them to turn red on the plant. According to Burpee, once daytime temperatures get into the 90s, tomatoes will only turn orange. If the heat is here to stay, let them ripen on your countertop. But if temps will break soon, just wait it out. You can pick them if a frost is coming or if animals are eating the fruit too.

MIDDLE, L-R: VAV63/GETTY IMAGES; MARTIN WIERINK/ALAMY STOCK PHOTO; BOTTOM, L-R: VADIM SHUMIAK, CHEERSGROUP/DREAMSTIME (2)

What's Your Best Veggie Hack?

Readers share their tried-and-true garden tips for growing fresh produce

Tomatoes

I add organic soil and crushed eggshells to the soil around my tomatoes, plus a thick layer of mulch to retain moisture and keep the ground warmer.

Jennifer Broadstreet Hess MARION, KS

I made a small square-foot-type garden with a mix of Black Gold soil, compost and something for drainage such as vermiculite. I only plant zucchini, another type of squash, Roma tomatoes and something new for fun each season. It wasn't inexpensive to start, but now I only need to enrich it each season. I harvest a ton from that small veggie garden—I even have some to give away.

Dawn Spero ENOLA, PA

Leave parsnips in the ground until after the first hard frost. They'll be sweeter.

Patricia Murray NILES, OH

Tomatoes require a lot of nutrients to grow, so I plant mine in pots. That way, it's easy to replenish the soil in the pot before each growing season.

Kathy Eppers ALEDO, TX

I plant beans in spring, then again in July, so we have some to harvest in October.

Nita Price LISBON, IA

To keep cabbage white caterpillars off my cabbage, I cover the plants with row covers or other season-extending fabrics.

Sharon Colden WARROAD, MN

Beans

TOMATOES: DUSTYPIXEL/GETTY IMAGES; BEANS: ID-VIDEO/SHUTTERSTOCK

How Do You Manage Bugs Naturally?

Say goodbye to pesky insects with these time-tested reader tips

Japanese beetles invade our garden every spring. I put a squirt of lemon Ajax dish soap and a cup of water in a pot, then knock the beetles into the pot.

Martha Russell CARMEL, ME

To keep slugs from eating tender young foliage, use horticultural-grade diatomaceous earth sprinkled around plants. Fresh herbs such as lemon balm also keep bad bugs away.

Kathy Eppers ALEDO, TX

To control ants, I sprinkle cinnamon along their trails and on their hills.

Jennifer Broadstreet Hess MARION, KS

Eastern bluebird

BLUEBIRD: ANEETA BROWN; VEGGIES: FLOORTJE/GETTY IMAGES

I'm a big fan of companion planting. One of my favorite combinations is alternating rows of carrots and onions. Together, they keep carrot flies and onion maggots away.

Sue Gronholz BEAVER DAM, WI

I grow mostly native trees, shrubs and perennials, and now the plants play host to certain insects that attract a variety of birds. It's a win-win that requires no management from me.

Sarah Miller AVONDALE ESTATES, GA

We put a bluebird house at the edge of our garden, and the birds manage the bugs for me. The plants lure the bugs, which are an easy meal for the bluebirds.

Monica Partington RALEIGH, NC

Grasses Galore

Add texture and grace to your space with picks in every size

By Wendy Helfenbaum

❮ Black mondo grass

OPHIOPOGON PLANISCAPUS 'NIGRESCENS', ZONES 6 TO 9

Add some drama to your garden with this dark purple-black grasslike perennial, which makes a bold border or ground cover. Arching mounded clumps produce pinkish white flowers in the summer and berries in the fall. This drought-tolerant, deer-resistant evergreen reaches 8 to 12 inches tall. It thrives in full sun and moist, well-draining soil.

Why we love it: Light foot traffic won't bother this plant.

^ Northern sea oats

CHASMANTHIUM LATIFOLIUM, ZONES 4 TO 9

Growing 3 to 4 feet tall, this native grass is known for its mass of hanging green seed heads that turn tan, then purplish. Sometimes called river oats, it does well in part shade or full sun in moist soil. Because northern sea oats tends to spread, it works best when planted in pots or in landscapes with room.

Why we love it: The seed heads produced by this low-maintenance grass can add whimsy to your floral arrangements.

^ Pink muhly grass

MUHLENBERGIA CAPILLARIS, ZONES 5 TO 9

For gardens with less-than-ideal soil, this graceful perennial grass delivers weeks of fall color. With branched blue-green foliage that reaches 2 to 4 feet tall, it does well as an edging or container plant. While this native grass tolerates part shade, you'll get the most vibrant color in full sun.

Why we love it: Birds love the large seed heads that remain after the fluffy pink and purple panicles fade.

MEXICAN FEATHER GRASS: RYZHKOV OLEKSANDR/SHUTTERSTOCK

❮ Mexican feather grass

NASSELLA TENUISSIMA, ZONES 7 TO 10

With late-summer tan blooms sitting atop delicate foliage, Mexican feather grass is a great choice for hot, dry gardens with plenty of sun. It's tolerant of many soils and is native to Texas and New Mexico, but it is invasive in California.

Why we love it: Give it a starring role in pots or in large swaths of hilly or sloped landscapes.

^ Dwarf pampas grass

CORTADERIA SELLOANA 'PUMILA', ZONES 5 TO 10

Come September, this 4-foot-tall grass produces fluffy, creamy silver-white plumes that make a statement at the back of borders. The flower heads then attract birds all winter long. Pampas grass is invasive in some states, so check before planting.

Why we love it: Both hardy and low-maintenance, this ornamental grass's feathery cuttings look great in floral arrangements.

^ Elijah Blue fescue

FESTUCA GLAUCA, ZONES 4 TO 8

Small but mighty, this 1-foot-tall grass features gorgeous powder-blue foliage in neat mounds. Requiring full sun or part shade in well-draining soil, it blossoms in early summer, but you'll be able to enjoy this drought-tolerant variety's bold color all year.

Why we love it: The unusual, cold-hardy blue stems look fabulous in container plantings or in masses.

› Zebra grass

MISCANTHUS SINENSIS 'ZEBRINUS', ZONES 5 TO 9

The name says it all: Each zebra grass leaf sports multiple light yellow horizontal stripes, which give this tall upright variety a showstopping presence. At 5 feet tall (or more!), it'll need room for its rounded, arching mound in full sun and moist, well-draining soil. Be sure to plant it where you can enjoy it all winter.

Why we love it: Rabbits and deer tend to leave it alone, and it is resistant to drought.

DWARF PAMPAS GRASS: OLGA SEIFUTDINOVA/GETTY IMAGES; ELIJAH BLUE FESCUE: BUTTERFLY'S DREAM/SHUTTERSTOCK;

^ Prairie Winds Desert Plains fountain grass

PENNISETUM ALOPECUROIDES, ZONES 5 TO 9

This variety stuns in a fall garden. It grows 3 to 4 feet tall in full sun. Its fluffy bottlebrush-shaped plumes start off with an impressive smoky purple color in early summer and age into a shade of tan in the fall.

Why we love it: Because Desert Plains fountain grass changes color through the months, it provides ongoing interest.

^ Graceful Grasses fiber optic grass

ISOLEPIS (SCIRPUS) CERNUA, ZONES 8 TO 10, ANNUAL ELSEWHERE

This compact, bright green, grasslike sedge grows up to a foot tall and can be planted in pots or as a filler in beds and borders. Beginning in early summer, it produces tiny, fuzzy white flowers.

Why we love it: Bring it indoors before the first frost and grow it as a houseplant.

‹ Creeping lilyturf

LIRIOPE SPICATA, ZONES 4 TO 10

Though technically not a grass, this plant's grasslike foliage makes it a good drought-tolerant ground cover. It spreads via rhizomes and is invasive in some states, so verify beforehand if it is a good pick for your area. Plant it in a bed with hardscaping to keep it confined.

Why we love it: Blue-black berries appear in fall, a treat for hungry birds.

FOUNTAIN GRASS, FIBER OPTIC GRASS: COURTESY OF PROVEN WINNERS - WWW.PROVENWINNERS (2); CREEPING LILYTURF: MELINDA MYERS LLC

Shrubs of All Sizes

Find the right choice for any space in your landscape

By Jodi Helmer

FEW LANDSCAPE ADDITIONS are more versatile than shrubs. A wide-ranging list of plants are on the market, including compact varieties ideal for borders and container gardens, medium-size specimens with a profusion of blooms, and larger species that offer shade or serve as windbreaks.

But it's not just the diversity of sizes that makes shrubs garden standouts. They can also provide habitat for wildlife, prevent erosion, add fragrance and complement an edible landscape—not to mention create a pleasing aesthetic.

Mountain laurel
Kalmia latifolia

PHOTOS FROM JAPAN, ASIA AND OTHE OF THE WORLD/GETTY IMAGES

SMALL SHRUBS

^ Annabelle hydrangea

HYDRANGEA ARBORESCENS, ZONES 3 TO 9

Hailed as one of the most popular landscape plants, this ornamental shrub grows 3 to 5 feet tall. A type of smooth hydrangea, Annabelle is best known for its massive round balls of white flowers that are profuse in summer and can even last into fall.

^ Creeping juniper

JUNIPERUS HORIZONTALIS, ZONES 3 TO 9

With a mature height of 18 inches or less, the evergreen plant forms dense mats that are ideal for rock gardens and slopes. The needles transition from green to purple tones in the winter.

^ New Jersey tea

CEANOTHUS AMERICANUS, ZONES 3 TO 9

This plant's leaves were used for tea during the American Revolution, and it's a host plant for spring and summer azure butterflies. It reaches a mature height of 2 to 3 feet and produces small white flowers starting in late spring.

› Kalm's St. John's wort

HYPERICUM KALMIANUM, ZONES 4 TO 7

In the summer, the shrub's golden yellow flowers add a welcome pop of color to the garden, and bees love them. The plant features bluish green leaves and grows 2 to 3 feet tall.

HYDRANGEA: WUT_MOPPIE/SHUTTERSTOCK; JUNIPER: VOLHA HALKOUSKAYA/GETTY IMAGES; TEA: BRYAN REYNOLDS; WORT: JAAP BLEIJENBERG/ALAMY STOCK PHOTO (2)

MEDIUM SHRUBS

› American elderberry

SAMBUCUS CANADENSIS, ZONES 4 TO 8

The dark purple fruits that appear in late summer are edible, and wildlife love to snack on them too. This shrub grows 6 to 12 feet tall, is tolerant of wetter soils and is also popular with animals for habitat.

^ Carolina allspice

CALYCANTHUS FLORIDUS, ZONES 4 TO 9

In sun or shade, this native shrub grows 6 to 10 feet tall. The hallmark maroon to reddish brown flowers have a sweet fruity fragrance.

^ Inkberry

ILEX GLABRA, ZONES 4 TO 9

Green-white flowers bloom in summer, and jet-black berries appear on female plants in winter if fertilized. This member of the holly family tolerates a wide range of soil conditions but prefers acidic soil, and it grows 5 to 10 feet tall.

^ Summersweet

CLETHRA ALNIFOLIA, ZONES 3 TO 9

Pollinators love the nectar from the spiky white or pink summer-blooming flowers. This shrub, native to the eastern United States, grows 3 to 5 feet tall on average but may reach up to 10 feet.

^ Virginia rose

ROSA VIRGINIANA, ZONES 3 TO 8

A low-maintenance shrub with a lovely scent, Virginia rose grows up to 6 feet tall and is popular with songbirds and native bees. It's covered with pretty pink flowers all summer long, and the rose hips are edible.

SUMMERSWEET: JOHN RICHMOND, ROSE: ALL CANADA PHOTOS/ALAMY STOCK PHOTO (2)

LARGE SHRUBS

^ Buttonbush

CEPHALANTHUS OCCIDENTALIS,
ZONES 5 TO 11

Thanks to a tolerance for wet soil and flood conditions, this native buttonbush makes an ideal addition to rain gardens. It can grow 12 feet tall, and pollinators are attracted to the pincushion-like flower heads that bloom in midsummer.

^ Common ninebark

PHYSOCARPUS OPULIFOLIUS,
ZONES 2 TO 8

This native plant's bark peels off in strips, revealing layers beneath. It's known as a winter interest shrub, but clusters of white or pinkish flowers in summer and bright yellow leaves in autumn give the 10-foot-tall shrub year-round appeal.

^ Highbush blueberry

VACCINIUM CORYMBOSUM,
ZONES 3 TO 8

This native blueberry species is found in bogs and swamps and grows well in moist, acidic soil. Some shrubs can grow up to 12 feet tall while producing delicious berries that can be eaten fresh or used in pies, jams and jellies.

› Mountain laurel

KALMIA LATIFOLIA,
ZONES 4 TO 9

This shade-tolerant plant grows 12 to 20 feet tall and is sometimes considered a small tree. Look for evergreen leaves and gorgeous clusters of hexagonal white to pink flowers with rose-colored spots on the inside. It is attractive to hummingbirds and pollinators and offers shelter for wildlife, but it should be noted that all parts are poisonous to humans if consumed.

BUTTONBUSH: ANDREAPAD77, NINEBARK: ALEXANDER DENISENKO/GETTY IMAGES (2); BLUEBERRY: SVETLANA ZHUKOVA/SHUTTERSTOCK; LAUREL: WILDNERDPIX, DOGWOOD: SKYSCAPES/GETTY IMAGES (2)

› Red twig dogwood

CORNUS SERICEA, ZONES 2 TO 7

The shrub, also called red osier, got its name for the red leaves and twigs that brighten up fall and winter landscapes. With a height of up to 10 feet and a tendency to form thickets, it's a great choice for a privacy screen.

Splendor in the Shade

Shadows won't stop these blooms from shining bright

By Peggy Riccio

Wedding Party Series

HELLEBORE: COURTESY OF PROVEN WINNERS - WWW.PROVENWINNERS; COLUMBINE: BALL HORTICULTURAL COMPANY;

Aquilegia Earlybird Purple White

‹ Hellebore

HELLEBORUS SPP., ZONES 4 TO 9

Deer-resistant hellebores thrive under deciduous shade trees or woodlands, in well-draining soil with lots of organic matter. These perennials bloom in the late winter and early spring with double or single flowers. Topping out at 2 feet, the glossy green foliage is largely evergreen in warmer climates.
Why we love it: Hellebores come in many colors and patterns such as spotted, speckled or dark-edged petals.

^ Columbine

AQUILEGIA SPP., ZONES 3 TO 8

Columbines are noted for nodding, pendulous blooms, rising above scalloped green foliage in late spring to early summer. Available in most colors and bicolor, too, these perennials are 1 to 3 feet tall, with equally attractive seed heads for dried flower arrangements.
Why we love it: The native eastern red columbine has delicate red and yellow flowers, attracting hummingbirds and other pollinators.

^ Carolina allspice

CALYCANTHUS FLORIDUS, ZONES 4 TO 9

A large native shrub, Carolina allspice blooms 2-inch-wide flowers from spring to summer. Varieties can have white, pink or red flowers with a strong fruity fragrance that attracts butterflies and pollinators. These deer-resistant shrubs, 6 to 10 feet tall and wide, prefer well-draining soil and tolerate moist locations.
Why we love it: The big flowers can be admired from the window or cut for fresh arrangements.

‹ Bleeding heart

DICENTRA SPECTABILIS, ZONES 3 TO 9

An old-fashioned spring ephemeral, bleeding heart blooms pink-and-white pendantlike flowers on thin, horizontal stems. The plant has delicate green foliage (although there is a golden form) that will reach several feet tall by late spring.
Why we love it: Bleeding heart is a tough, long-lasting perennial that comes back each year.

Pink Champagne

^ Black cohosh

ACTAEA RACEMOSA, ZONES 3 TO 8

A native perennial, black cohosh grows to about 4 to 6 feet tall and blooms spikes of tiny creamy white flowers high above the astilbe-like foliage. Deer-resistant black cohosh prefers rich, well-draining soil in medium shade and can be grown under hardwood trees.

Why we love it: The summer flowers are sweetly scented, attracting pollinating flies, beetles and bees.

^ Barrenwort

EPIMEDIUM SPP., ZONES 4 TO 9

In the late spring to early summer, barrenwort blooms delicate flowers suspended on thin stems. Available in many colors, each blossom is shaped like a four-corner hat or a spider. This perennial ground cover has heart- or arrow-shaped foliage, which can change to red or bronze in the fall.

Why we love it: Durable and tolerant of dry soil, it is ideal for planting under trees.

› Bugbane

ACTAEA SIMPLEX, ZONES 4 TO 8

Preferring moist, well-draining soil, bugbane is a perennial with green or dark foliage varieties. Spikes of small, fragrant, creamy white flowers bloom in late summer and can reach 4 to 6 feet tall. The flower petals are slightly fringed, creating a bottlebrush effect.

Why we love it: The pale, delicate flowers are even more dramatic against the dark foliage, which goes well with light-colored plants.

BLACK COHOSH: GIOREZ/GETTY IMAGES; BARRENWORT, INDIAN PINK: WALTERS GARDENS, INC (2);

^ Indian pink

SPIGELIA MARILANDICA, ZONES 5 TO 9

This plant has bright red tubular flowers with yellow tips at the opening of each tube. Indian pink prefers moist, well-draining soil high in organic matter. Individual plants are only about 1 foot wide, so plant several for a show from late spring to summer.

Why we love it: Indian pink is a striking native perennial plant, attracting hummingbirds.

^ Hardy begonia

BEGONIA GRANDIS, ZONES 6 TO 9

From summer to fall, hardy begonia has typical pink begonia flowers clustered on long, slender pink stems. Relatively bushy, this perennial is 1 to 3 feet tall and prefers rich, moist and well-draining soil.

Why we love it: The red backsides of the leaves have a stained-glass appearance when lit from the back.

ASTILBE: COURTESY OF PROVEN WINNERS - WWW.PROVENWINNERS

‹ Astilbe

ASTILBE SPP., ZONES 3 TO 9

Although many varieties are 1 to 4 feet tall, astilbes look even taller when large plumes of feathery flowers bloom in red, pink, maroon or white. Preferring moist but well-draining soil, astilbes have fernlike foliage in green or bronze color.

Why we love it: These perennials add a pretty, bright punch of color all summer long and look great in large containers.

Easiest Hydrangea Ever

Pro tips for proper panicle care

By Jodi Helmer

SOME TYPES OF HYDRANGEAS CAN BE FICKLE. They can be prone to pests and diseases; excess sun burns their leaves; and overwatering or underwatering may cause them to die. But panicle hydrangeas (*Hydrangea paniculata*) offer an easier-to-grow option.

The plants, sometimes called peegee or hardy hydrangeas, produce pretty single-petal flowers on pyramidal heads, in contrast to the hallmark mophead flowers on bigleaf hydrangeas. "They make a big splash in the garden," says Lorraine Ballato, horticulturist and author of *Success with Hydrangeas*. "They contribute a tremendous amount to the vibrancy of the garden."

Narrow the Options

One thing gardeners love about panicle hydrangeas is the diversity. Lorraine notes that traditional bigleaf hydrangeas were primarily pink and blue, but panicles offer flowers that change colors as the blooms mature.

"Now you can get these wowie-zowie colors," Lorraine says. Fire Light features large, full mophead flowers that are creamy white when they emerge and gradually transform into a vivid red hue. Pinky Winky is known for its large white panicles that transition to a pretty shade of pink in the fall. Candy Apple boasts compact lime green flower clusters.

Color is just one of the features to consider when choosing panicle hydrangeas. Lorraine suggests considering size too. Some dwarf varieties are under 3 feet, while some full-sized plants grow up to 8 feet tall or more and just as wide.

Limelight

COURTESY OF PROVEN WINNERS - WWW.PROVENWINNERS (4)

Pinky Winky panicle hydrangea

Get Growing

Panicle hydrangeas grow well in Zones 3 to 9. Plant them in a sunny spot (with afternoon shade in hot climates) and well-draining soil. Minimal fertilization is needed. A soil test can help you determine proper fertilization needs.

Thanks to their hardiness, panicle hydrangeas are ideal for container gardening. Choose durable and weatherproof containers and provide extra winter protection if you're in a colder climate. Repot into larger pots every three years as the plant matures.

Prioritize Pruning

Minimal annual pruning during the dormant season can be done if needed to promote stem strength and help you control the size and shape of the plant. Since panicle hydrangeas flower on new growth, it's safe to prune them in early spring before the leaves appear or in late fall after the leaves have fallen, says Lorraine.

Why Pick Panicles

If you want to grow hydrangeas, hardy, low-maintenance panicles are a good alternative to bigleaf types. Benefits include reliable blooms, an array of color choices and drought tolerance.

Fire Light

Zinfin Doll

Candy Apple

CANDY APPLE: MONROVIA BY DOREENWYNJA.COM

Hydrangea Facts

Get to know the highlights of this beloved family

By Jill Staake

Let's Dance Sky View hydrangea

1999 **In 1999, Alabama designated the oakleaf hydrangea as its state wildflower.**

6 Hundreds of hydrangea species and cultivars exist, but the six most common types are bigleaf, oakleaf, panicle, smooth, mountain and climbing.

2 Bigleaf hydrangeas have two types of blooms: large, showy mopheads, and lacecaps that sport tiny budlike florets surrounded by larger blooms.

5.5 Not all hydrangeas change color, but those that can are blue when the soil pH is below 5.5 and pink when the pH is 6 or higher.

3 Panicle hydrangeas tend to be the most cold tolerant, with varieties that are hardy in Zone 3.

30 With the right support and conditions, climbing hydrangeas grow 30 feet tall or more.

COURTESY OF PROVEN WINNERS - WWW.PROVENWINNERS

Mighty Milkweed

What to know about this butterfly garden staple

By Jill Staake

Monarch butterfly on milkweed

Prostrate milkweed

LEFT: RICHARD DAY/DAYBREAK IMAGERY; RIGHT: JOEY SANTORE/CRIME PAYS BUT BOTANY DOESN'T

140 More than 140 species of milkweed (*Asclepias* spp.) are found in nature.

1 Milkweed is the one and only host plant for monarchs, which prefer local, native varieties.

2 Though monarchs are the most well known, two other orange-and-black butterflies in the United States use milkweed as a host plant: queens and soldiers.

24 Prostrate milkweed (*A. prostrata*) is endangered, with only 24 populations remaining in South Texas and northern Mexico.

48 The lower 48 states (and nine Canadian provinces) have native milkweed species to choose from.

5 Milkweed flowers typically have five downward-facing petals, and an upward-facing corona made up of five hoods.

40 The floss from two bags of ripe milkweed pods (40 lbs. total) could fill one life jacket for World War II sailors.

Bees enjoy stopping by Phenomenal lavender.

DIANA ROBINSON PHOTOGRAPHY/GETTY IMAGES

Grow Backyard Lavender

This fragrant perennial can thrive in many areas of the country

By Luke Miller

LAVENDER IS ONE of the best-known plants—if not by sight, then by smell. It's hard to argue with the beauty of its fragrance, silver-gray foliage and spiky flowers—which, as you might suspect, are often lavender-colored, although purple, pink and white blooms are also available.

Native to rocky hillsides in the Mediterranean, lavender prefers hot, dry summers and cool, moist winters, so it's right at home on Donna Anderson's Lavender Acres farm in Meridian, Idaho. But it can be grown elsewhere if the conditions are right. In addition to six to 10 hours of sunlight, lavender needs lighter, well-draining alkaline soil and special care when watering.

"Many homeowners will put lavender in their landscaping and let the lawn sprinklers water it," Donna says. But, she points out, grass requires a lot more water than lavender does, and too much water can kill the fragrant plant.

Small, bushy and a perennial, lavender grows 1 to 3 feet tall, depending on the species or cultivar. The plant has three main types: English, English hybrids and non-English, which include Spanish, French, sweet and woolly. Their winter hardiness varies between categories. Count on French lavender (*Lavandula stoechas*)

to thrive in Zones 8 to 10, while English lavender (*L. angustifolia*) can take the colder temperatures of Zones 5 to 9.

Once your lavender is established well, it is quite low maintenance, requiring only an annual trim to encourage growth and keep it tidy. "Depending on the location of the lavender, you can prune in the fall if it is pruned at least six weeks before heavy frost," Donna says. If you live in an area with harsh winters, prune in late March or April.

Although lavender can be grown in many parts of the country, Donna suggests doing some research before starting out. "There are tiny microclimates in all areas, so a lavender variety that grows well for one grower might not grow as well for another 5 miles away," she says. Always reach out to your local nursery or university extension for their recommendations.

Growing Indoors

If lavender isn't reliably winter hardy in your area, you may be able to overwinter it indoors before bringing it back outside in warmer weather. Overwinter it in a large pot placed in a cool room. Other things to consider:

LIGHTING: Lavender needs plenty of bright, natural lighting, so place it near a south-facing window.

SOIL: Use a lightweight potting mix augmented with sand and gravel in a quick-draining terra-cotta pot. Test the soil and add limestone if the pH result is found to be below 7.

WATERING: Wet the plant's base only, not the leaves or blooms. For best results, allow the soil to dry out slightly between waterings.

Best Picks for Your Region

Find the perfect type of lavender for your yard.

Southeast
- Grosso, French hybrid
- Munstead, English
- Provence, French
- Spanish types

Pacific Northwest
- Folgate, English
- Royal Velvet, English
- Super, English hybrid
- Violet Intrigue, English

Northeast and Midwest
- Hidcote, English
- Munstead, English
- Sachet, English

Southwest
- Grosso, French hybrid

Succulents for Pollinators

Discover drought-tolerant plants that provide nectar for bees, butterflies and birds

By Alice Knisley Matthias

Blooming hens-and-chicks

SOMETIMES OVERLOOKED as wildlife-friendly, succulents grown in the garden do attract bees, birds and butterflies. It's easy to offer the plants to pollinators—simply find ones that are hardy for your area or bloom during a time of year that you can keep them outside. Provide an abundance of color, flower shapes, heights and scents for the best chance of attracting pollinators to succulents. Try these top picks!

Hens-and-Chicks

Widely available at most garden centers and a favorite go-to addition in the garden, hens-and-chicks are named for the rosette shape that grows at the center of the plant and its numerous small offspring. The star-shaped blooms attract bees and butterflies. This is a super reliable, hardy choice for those just starting to plant succulents outdoors.

Echeveria

Echeveria is an easy-to-care-for outdoor succulent. This variety will do well in a garden landscape and is also a solid option for planting in pots. Gardeners tend to use this plant for its leaf color, which can create pleasing visuals in a mixture of plantings. The arching flowers of echeveria are favored by pollinators such as hummingbirds, bees and butterflies.

Crassula

Talk to gardeners who work with succulents, and they will tell you that crassula's appeal is how easy it is to care for and that it grows well in both decorative pots and the garden bed. A few popular options in this group are jade plant, money tree or friendship plant. The plants form clusters of wispy flowers that have a light, sweet scent favored by bees.

Kalanchoe

Many people are fans of kalanchoe as a houseplant, but it can be a colorful accent outside too. These plants are fairly drought tolerant, but monitor their water needs, as a lack of water can stunt the

Arrow echeveria

Crassula

Kalanchoe

ECHEVERIA, ICE PLANT, SEDUM: COURTESY OF PROVEN WINNERS - WWW.PROVENWINNERS.COM (3); CRASSULA: MAGICFLUTE002, HENS-AND-CHICKS: RUDOLF VLCEK,

Fire Spinner ice plant

Haworthia

development of the brightly hued flowers. The plant produces tiny seeds after flowering.

Trailing Ice Plant

Honeybees will be sure to visit your succulent garden if you grow ice plant (*Delosperma*), which provides abundant sources of nectar. It grows colorful 1- to 3-inch-wide flowers that make a showy display in the landscape and provide visual interest as well as a place for pollinators to perch.

Pride and Joy sedum

Sedum

One of the first plants to emerge when the garden springs back to life, sedum will thrive well into the fall season. Bees, birds and butterflies are happy to stop by for a visit on the clusters of tiny star-shaped flowers. Sedum is available in many varieties and pretty colors, ranging from bold garnet to soft pinks. Try ground cover types such as John Creech, Album and Dragon's Blood, which are known to be wildlife friendly.

Haworthia

Haworthoria provides a display of colorful foliage if you have an area that gets a bit of shade from a fence or cover from larger bushes. Haworthoria's tubular blooms are either pink or white, and several sit on a single stem, making them an interesting stop for bees and butterflies in search of food.

Pollinator Power

Many succulents are pollinated primarily by animals. Besides the usual birds, butterflies and bees, succulents get help from moths and bats too.

Show Off Your Succulents

Eight easy ways to make the water-saving plants stand out in the garden

By Luke Miller

A hollow log is a gorgeous DIY planter.

SUCCULENTS HAVE BEEN POPULAR HOUSEPLANTS FOR YEARS, and for good reason. They are easy to care for and come in a wide range of colors, shapes and sizes. Here are eight ways to let them shine outside.

1. Decorate a Fence

Top a fence or wall with planter boxes and let succulents such as burro's tail or string of pearls trail downward to soften the structure and add visual interest.

2. Make a Mosaic

With so much variety, succulents are ready to be mixed and matched into any design or pattern. Combine different types to create a mosaic. Be creative with your plants and arrangements. Geometric and abstract designs both look great. You can also throw in cactuses (which prefer the same growing conditions) for extra texture.

3. Arrange a Potted Vignette

Succulents do great in containers, but the plants are sometimes too small to carry visual interest from a distance. That's when it pays to group plants in color-coordinated vessels so they look like one cohesive unit. Repeat your chosen hue and mix up the heights and sizes of the pots for more appeal. You can include a darker accent container to add depth.

4. Plant a Ground Cover

Outdoor succulents are known to make outstanding drought-tolerant ground covers. Pick one that's hardy in your area—Angelina sedum or hens-and-chicks grow in many places. The plants save time and effort once they're established, and provide much more color and

LEFT: OLGA_PRAVA/GETTY IMAGES; RIGHT, FROM TOP: COURTESY OF PROVEN WINNERS - WWW.PROVENWINNERS.COM; KYNNY/GETTY IMAGES; KORKAI/SHUTTERSTOCK.COM

dimension to your landscape than traditional grass.

5. Create a Miniature Garden

Plant a miniature fairy garden to enjoy up close. Most of these gardens are small enough to be portable, so you can plant one in a container and move it wherever you want. Maybe it's a centerpiece for an outdoor party that later sits on the porch. Plus you can take it indoors to a bright and sunny location if cold weather is on the way.

6. Fill a Worry-Free Window Box

Sure, we've all forgotten to water a window box at some point. And we've all paid the price with dead—or at least mightily struggling—plants. Here's where succulents come to the rescue. They can go a week or more between waterings, depending on the conditions, so they'll still look fresh even if their irrigation is irregular for a spell.

7. Rock On With a Rock Garden

Succulents should be a part of every rock garden—if not the main attraction. Thanks to their drought-tolerant nature, they are naturally adapted to the hot, sunny conditions and the lean soil of traditional rock gardens. Many succulents will creep and slowly cover the stone, while others will stay small and fill little pockets.

8. Have a Ball

A precast concrete sphere with holes of various sizes can be filled with potting mix and an assortment of succulents. Similar products to the one shown below can be found in garden centers, or you can make your own. Drill holes into a bowling ball or globe, or shape chicken wire and coco liner into a round planter.

Angelina sedum

Mix different succulents for an eclectic centerpiece.

A concrete sphere with sedum, Pachyphytum and elephant bush

Ready for the Heat

Fill your summer garden with water-wise picks

By Wendy Helfenbaum

Multiple Benefits

Beyond its ability to attract pollinators, amethyst sea holly is easy to grow and resists salt damage.

‹ Amethyst sea holly

ERYNGIUM AMETHYSTINUM, ZONES 3 TO 9

Eye-catching and compact, sea holly has spiny gray-green foliage and prickly cool blue flower heads that bloom in mid-to-late summer. This deer-resistant plant loves hot sun and well-draining soil but will survive just about anywhere. Add this sea holly to borders or a cutting garden.

Why we love it: Bees and butterflies flock to this plant's blooms, which also shine quite well in floral arrangements.

^ Moss rose

PORTULACA GRANDIFLORA, ANNUAL

A member of the purslane family, moss rose grows to create a mat that is 3 to 8 inches high and up to 1 foot wide. It makes for a stunning spiller in a hanging planter. Give it full sun—the flowers open only in sunlight before closing in the evening. Try the Fairy Tale series for pompomlike flowers or Sundial for blooms that stay open longer during the day.

Why we love it: The petals have a ruffled appearance and come in a wide array of colors.

^ Rosemary

SALVIA ROSMARINUS, ZONES 7 TO 11 OR ANNUAL

A fragrant evergreen shrub that also serves as a savory herb, rosemary has needlelike leaves and clusters of flowers in pale blue to white that bloom from late winter through summer. Growing up to 6 feet tall, it requires moist, well-draining soil and full sun for best results. Prune if desired after flowering.

Why we love it: You can keep it in a pot indoors to overwinter or for easy additions to recipes.

‹ Gold Nugget hens-and-chicks

SEMPERVIVUM, ZONES 4 TO 9

Provide a year-round display of vibrant color with Gold Nugget. The succulent's foliage changes from lime green in summer to golden red during cooler months. Place it in gritty, well-draining soil where the plant can receive full sun or very light shade.

Why we love it: With low-growing rosettes that spread 6 to 8 inches, hens-and-chicks can be easily divided by pulling out a few chicks (smaller rosettes) and replanting.

ROSEMARY: JASENKA ARBANAS/GETTY IMAGES (2); GOLD NUGGET: LITTLE PRINCE OF OREGON NURSERY/WWW.LITTLEPRINCEPLANTS.COM

^ Pineleaf penstemon

PENSTEMON PINIFOLIUS, ZONES 4 TO 9

Native to the southern Rocky Mountains, this compact perennial features foliage that resembles pine needles and has tubular flowers with bright red, orange and yellow tones. Also known as beardtongue, penstemon loves full sun and is a magnet for bees, hummingbirds and other helpful pollinators.

Why we love it: Deer leave it alone. Plus it's easy to grow on slopes or in rock gardens.

^ Red creeping thyme

THYMUS PRAECOX 'COCCINEUS', ZONES 3 TO 8

Creeping thyme is a drought-tolerant ground cover with a bounty of blooms. Many thyme varieties do well with very little water, but this magenta-hued version is especially vibrant and fragrant. Keep it in full or part sun. Tuck clusters into rock gardens or near walls, where they will spread 8 to 12 inches.

Why we love it: The dark foliage slowly transforms to a beautiful bronze color during fall.

› Color Guard Adam's needle

YUCCA FILAMENTOSA, ZONES 4 TO 10

This desert plant has spiked variegated foliage and ivory bell-shaped flowers that appear on 4-to-6-foot stalks in midsummer. It's a striking focal point in a low-water garden. Put it in a spot with sunshine and well-draining soil, and the plant will easily grow 2 to 3 feet wide. Find it at an online retailer such as Monrovia.

Why we love it: Color Guard is salt tolerant, does well as a container plant and attracts hummingbirds, but deer tend to leave it be.

PINELEAF PENSTEMON: HIGHCOUNTRYGARDENS.COM; CREEPING THYME, BUTTERFLY WEED: COURTESY OF PROVEN WINNERS - WWW.PROVENWINNERS (2)

^ Butterfly weed

ASCLEPIAS TUBEROSA, ZONES 3 TO 9

This bushy perennial is known for its showstopping clusters of vivid flowers that bloom throughout the summer. Add it to a cottage garden with easy access for cut flowers. The seedpods add texture and interest to a dried floral arrangement, and it will self-seed if pods aren't removed.

Why we love it: Butterflies adore it, and monarchs use it as a host plant.

^ Arizona Sun blanket flower

GAILLARDIA, ZONES 3 TO 9

Requiring little water and suitable in small spaces, this easy-to-grow perennial forms a swath of deep red, orange and yellow daisylike blossoms. Arizona Sun, an All-America Selections winner sold by Monrovia and other producers, prefers full sun and well-draining soil, and it beautifully tolerates heat.

Why we love it: A long-lasting bloomer, it flowers from early summer to fall. Deadhead to extend the color show.

‹ Cascade stonecrop

SEDUM DIVERGENS, ZONES 2 TO 9

This succulent's tightly stacked, plump leaves range from green to darker red. Golden, star-shaped flowers appear in summer. Also known as spreading stonecrop, it's a tough, low-maintenance plant that needs lots of sunlight but very little water.

Why we love it: Use this fast-growing plant as a ground cover or to enhance rock gardens, borders and containers.

Foolproof Ferns

It's time to shine a well-deserved spotlight on these shade-happy, no-fuss garden superstars

By Luke Miller

Interrupted fern

FERNS DESERVE MORE ATTENTION in landscaping discussions. They're far outnumbered by hostas and other shade plants at local nurseries—and, perhaps as a result, homeowners tend to overlook these ancient inhabitants of the forest. But home gardeners who haven't discovered the benefits of ferns are missing out!

Layers of Texture

Thriving in full to part shade, ferns flourish where many other plants struggle. "Most of them have such a fine texture," says Alan Branhagen, director of operations at the Minnesota Landscape Arboretum. "Few other plants have such delicate, intricate leaflets and divided-up fronds—ferns just create a lot of interest and detail."

Give Wildlife a Boost

As a naturalist with an interest in botany, butterflies and birds, Alan appreciates the main benefit that ferns provide to wildlife. "Ferns don't produce seeds or anything that birds eat," he says, "but they provide good habitat for soil invertebrates and, in that respect, they are really good in a woodland garden for ground-feeding birds."

He notes that he sometimes sees warblers hopping around on the forest floor under ferns. "A lot of our thrushes—from robins to the migrant thrushes that go up north—really like that sort of

DOREENWYNJA.COM PHOTOGRAPHY

habitat to scratch around in," Alan says.

Fern TLC

To maximize the value of deciduous ferns, let their foliage die back on its own. "They don't have big twiggy stems, so they compost themselves pretty readily," says Alan. After a freeze, he suggests letting ferns become mulch, which will support earthworms, spiders and other helpful garden critters.

Deer occasionally browse on ferns, but not as their first choice. Slugs and other insects aren't normally a problem either. "Ferns are pretty low maintenance," Alan says. "They're an ancient group of plants and they've been around a long, long time. There just really aren't many issues as long as you choose a fern that is hardy for your zone and put it in conditions that it likes."

Pair 'Em Up

For the best and biggest visual effect, group ferns together in flowing designs inside a natural garden. "They pair well with azaleas in high shade or underneath small woodland trees," Alan says.

Other fern companions Alan recommends include wood poppy, bloodroot, jack-in-the-pulpit, Canadian wild ginger and European wild ginger.

He also particularly likes planting ferns with spring ephemerals, such as Virginia bluebells. He says, "By June they are fading away, and that's when the ferns come up and fill the space."

Giant wood fern

Ostrich fern

Japanese painted fern

SELECTING FERNS

Carefully choose a fern species to fit your available space. Here are some of Alan Branhagen's recommendations.

Ferns for Large Spaces

GIANT WOOD FERN (*Dryopteris goldieana*), Zones 3 to 8. It grows 3 to 4 feet tall, and it looks fantastic as a specimen plant or massed in woodland gardens along ponds or streams.

INTERRUPTED FERN (*Osmunda claytoniana*), Zones 3 to 8. Typically 3 or 4 feet tall in most gardens but can tower to a dramatic 6 feet when it's happy.

OSTRICH FERN (*Matteuccia struthiopteris*), Zones 3 to 8. Make a big garden statement with this 3-to-5-foot-tall giant of the fern world.

ROYAL FERN (*Onoclea struthiopteris*), Zones 3 to 10. This native thrives in partially shaded areas that tend to have wet soil.

Ferns for Small Spaces

JAPANESE HOLLY FERN (*Cyrtomium falcatum*),

GIANT WOOD: PAUL M. DZIUK; OSTRICH: FLOWERPHOTOS/UNIVERSAL IMAGES GROUP VIA GETTY IMAGES; JAPANESE PAINTED: LYNN GEDEON/SHUTTERSTOCK

Northern maidenhair fern

Top Care Tips

- Plant ferns in fall or early spring so they establish before the heat of summer.
- Find a shady spot. Mild morning light is fine, but their foliage burns in hot afternoon sun.
- Add compost to promote the soil's health.
- Water well throughout their first growing season—many ferns can become drought tolerant once established.

Zones 6 to 10. It's rarely more than 2 feet tall and has particularly shiny evergreen leaves.

JAPANESE PAINTED FERN (*Athyrium niponicum* var. *pictum*), Zones 3 to 8. Growing just 12 to 18 inches tall and wide, its intricate patterns add a dimension of color to landscapes.

NORTHERN MAIDENHAIR FERN (*Adiantum hispidulum*), Zones 3 to 8 and southern maidenhair fern (*Adiantum capillus-veneris*), Zones 6 to 9. Delicate and small, the leaves of these two options provide some texture in a shade garden.

Royal fern

Japanese holly fern

Interrupted fern

MAIDENHAIR: PHOTO COURTESY OF THE MINNESOTA LANDSCAPE ARBORETUM; ROYAL: FEDSAX/GETTY IMAGES; JAPANESE HOLLY: ARTUR BOGACKI, INTERRUPTED: NOMISH/ALAMY STOCK PHOTO (2)

CHAPTER 3

Fall

Who says autumn's just bare branches and sleepy blooms? Celebrate the changing season with our tried-and-true backyard tips to keep your garden going through the cold.

Flowing into Fall

Plan a landscape that flourishes beyond just spring and summer for a space both you and the visiting wildlife will love

By Luke Miller

GREG RYAN/ALAMY STOCK PHOTO

AS PEAK GROWING SEASON WINDS DOWN, it's time to think about extending your garden's interest into fall. Discounted plants are abundant this time of the year, and birds will certainly be thankful for additional sustenance and shelter. Plus, cool-weather landscaping can absolutely still be beautiful.

After four decades of designing and installing gardens, Darryl Abraham of Naples, New York, appreciates options that aren't just easy on the eyes but also on the back. "I'm on the naturalizing, low-maintenance side of things," he says.

He also knows the value of working in layers and using a variety of plants—trees, shrubs, grasses, flowers and ground covers—for contrast in height, shape and texture. Some of his favorite fall plants include red twig dogwood, gray dogwood, rose of Sharon, ornamental grasses, goldenrod, milkweed and American bittersweet.

Darryl is an advocate for autumn gardens thanks in part to his parents, garden authors and radio hosts George "Doc" and Katy Abraham. They grew lush landscapes that included hazelnut shrubs, brambles, apple trees and more—for their own enjoyment and to help sustain wildlife.

To design a gorgeous outdoor space with lasting power, follow some of Darryl's top fall plant recommendations.

Great Grasses

Ornamental grasses peak after summer, when they reach their mature height and develop striking flower heads. Many turn an attractive buff color, which serves as a perfect backdrop for bright companions such as mums and sedums.

Combine ornamental grasses, asters and maple trees to create a bold autumn look.

Bumblebee visiting coneflower

And a few offer their own hues, such as flame grass (*Miscanthus* 'Purpurascens'), which turns a fiery red-orange.

Most grasses remain upright during the cooler months, adding extended interest. Darryl says, "They'll go right through the winter, have kind of a brown tuft, and then you cut them back in the spring and get the new growth coming out. They're fairly easy to maintain."

Appealing Fruits

Certain fruitful plants attract birds in autumn, including mountain ash, a favorite of cedar and Bohemian waxwings. Other seasonal picks that get a thumbs-up from Darryl include American bittersweet, blackberries, cotoneaster and sumac, with its beautiful burgundy leaves in fall and conical fruiting structures.

Standout Shrubs and Trees

When it comes to adding trees and shrubs with flair, Darryl recommends mock orange and viburnum, which offer spring flowers and striking fall foliage. Rose of Sharon blooms from summer into early fall. And hydrangeas have large summer flowers that fade into attractive tones of pink and tan. Look to oakleaf hydrangea (*Hydrangea quercifolia*) for burgundy fall foliage.

As for trees, Darryl suggests both red or sugar maples for some brilliant fall foliage color and northern catalpa (*Catalpa speciosa*) for its cigar-shaped seedpods.

Fall Flowers

While mums are a well-known seasonal standout, Darryl likes seed-bearing perennials that feed birds. He says, "Black-eyed Susans are pretty

FROM LEFT: MELISSA BELLER; ROLFNUSSBAUMER.COM;

Black-crested titmouse at a bigtooth maple

tough, and echinacea is another good one." Other favorites of his include Joe Pye weed and asters. Leave the flowers standing or break up the seed heads and cast them around for the birds.

Evergreen Beauties

"Birds pretty much like any kind of tree," Darryl says. But he points out that they tend to especially enjoy the shelter of evergreens.

Some good options to plant include western redcedar (*Thuja plicata*), eastern redcedar (*Juniperus virginiana*), Chinese juniper (*Juniperus chinensis*) and blue spruce (*Picea pungens*). For long-term success, make sure the trees you select are suitable for your growing conditions and are noninvasive for your area.

With the right picks and planning, it's easy to set up your garden for enjoyment well into fall.

Potted Combos

Mix and match autumn plants that love containers.

- Chrysanthemums
- Coleus
- Coral bells
- Creeping Jenny
- Dusty miller
- Marigolds
- Melampodium
- Ornamental kale
- Pansies
- Petunias
- Purple fountain grass
- Sedges
- Zinnias

8 Never-Skip Garden Tips

Master gardeners share simple steps to set you up for success

By Mikayla Borchert

1. Test Soil

Choose plants, fertilizers and soil amendments without the guesswork. Simple, inexpensive soil tests reveal exactly what you need. At-home soil test kits are one option. However, Charlotte Ekker Wiggins, a University of Missouri Extension master gardener emeritus and author, recommends that you contact a local university extension office. She says they offer easy, reliable soil sample testing that includes recommendations of how to amend soil for your desired greenery.

2. Provide Space

It's easy to buy too many plants or to overcrowd them, but that can lead to an unruly or unmanageable garden. "Planting plants without room around them to grow can overtax the soil of nutrients, resulting in less-than-healthy plants," Charlotte says.

Haeley Giambalvo, a certified Texas master naturalist and member of the Texas Native Plant Society, says, "Spacing correctly from the get-go can save a lot of time and headaches down the road by avoiding having to reposition or remove plants that have overgrown their space."

3. Fertilize Sparingly

Most plants don't need to be fertilized as often as you might

FROM LEFT: STURTI, FOTOMEM/GETTY IMAGES (2)

Layer green and brown materials for the best compost.

think. Some fertilizers can have a negative effect, causing plants to become leggy or to produce less fruit. Charlotte recommends slow-release granular fertilizers for most new gardeners.

4. Compost Carefully

Compost is one of the best organic soil amendments—and you can make it for free! It's good for the environment too. "Approximately 40% of all food in the United States is tossed out," says Charlotte. "Put it to good use restoring the soil that grows our food."

5. Honor Hardiness

It's possible to grow plants from other climates as annuals, but be selective.

"It can be tempting to buy one of every pretty flower you see in full bloom at the nursery," Haeley says. "Many nursery flowers are native to other parts of the globe and require special care and babying to thrive in your climate." For that reason, research your exact hardiness zone and choose plants that are suitable for your climate.

6. Water Mindfully

Plants need moisture, but watering too often can cause root rot and other diseases. Research how much water each plant needs to keep it hydrated well.

Young outdoor plants need consistent, regular watering. "Even the hardiest of plants need time to adjust to their new location once they've been transplanted," Haeley says. Give them plenty of frequent moisture at first, then taper off watering as their roots develop.

7. Match the Conditions

When designing your landscaping, consider more than aesthetics. Monitor the planting area and note how many hours of direct sunlight it gets throughout the day. Research plants that fit the light conditions, and always check the label before impulse buying at the garden center.

8. Get Help Weeding

Once a garden is planted, weeding becomes an endless chore—don't do all the work yourself! Rely on prep work to reduce unwanted plants.

"I like to create a weed barrier by lining a garden bed with flattened cardboard boxes, then covering with a few inches of wood mulch," Haeley says. This method also helps the soil retain moisture, which creates happier, healthier plants.

Autumn Superstars

Welcome shorter days and longer nights with colorful perennials that light up your late-season garden

By Melinda Myers

Pollinator Approved
Hummingbirds and butterflies, like this pipevine swallowtail, go crazy for the nectar of Alma Potschke aster.

ASTER: RICHARD DAY/DAYBREAK IMAGERY; GARDEN MUM: DOREENWYNJA.COM;

‹ Alma Potschke aster

SYMPHYOTRICHUM NOVAE-ANGLIAE 'ANDENKEN AN ALMA POTSCHKE,' ZONES 4 TO 8

Vivid rose-pink blooms on this New England aster grab the attention of passersby. Pinch the stems back to 6 inches throughout June to encourage compact growth, sturdier stems and more flowers. Or let it grow (it'll reach about 4 feet) and surround it with sturdy neighbors. **Why we love it:** Birds and butterflies visit this beauty, which adds motion and life to your yard.

^ Mammoth garden mum

CHRYSANTHEMUM MORIFOLIUM 'MAMMOTH,' ZONES 3 TO 9

Bred by the University of Minnesota, this hardy mum is right at home in both the north and south. Grow it in full sun in the garden or a container. This heavy bloomer produces plenty of flowers, so share fresh-from-the-garden bouquets with friends. **Why we love it:** It's a large mum that needs no early season pinching to stand upright in your autumn garden.

^ Fireworks goldenrod

SOLIDAGO RUGOSA 'FIREWORKS,' ZONES 4 TO 9

An explosion of bright yellow flowers tops this 3-foot plant. Grow low-maintenance Fireworks in full sun or light shade. Contrary to popular belief, this is not the hay fever culprit. Ragweed, which is often found growing next to goldenrod, causes the sniffles. **Why we love it:** Goldenrods are a great nectar and pollen source for fall's flying pollinators and other beneficial insects.

‹ Lemon Queen sunflower

HELIANTHUS 'LEMON QUEEN,' ZONES 4 TO 9

Save a spot in the back of the garden for this royal sunflower. Creamy yellow flowers top 6-foot-tall plants from late summer through fall. The upright, bushy plant provides a nice backdrop for neighboring flowers. Pinch the stems back throughout June if you want to keep your plant shorter. **Why we love it:** It's great as a cut flower. Plus, hummingbirds and butterflies take advantage of the bright blooms.

^ Joe Pye weed

EUTROCHIUM PURPUREUM, ZONES 4 TO 9

Give this big boy some room! It reaches 7 feet tall in full sun to partial shade and moist soil. You and the butterflies will fall in love with the large, fragrant mauve-pink flower clusters. Plus, the seed heads persist and add texture to your winter garden.

Why we love it: For tight spaces, try Little Joe (3 to 4 feet tall) and Baby Joe (32 inches tall). Both of these small options are ideal for rain gardens.

^ Russian sage

PEROVSKIA ATRIPLICIFOLIA, ZONES 4 TO 9

Blue flowers shine from summer through fall on this stunning heat- and drought-tolerant plant. Grow it in full sun and well-draining soil for best results. Prune plants back to 4 inches in late winter or early spring for more compact growth. Or grow a compact variety such as Blue Spires, Lacey Blue or Denim 'n Lace.

Why we love it: The fragrant foliage adds a bit of aromatherapy to your spring garden cleanup.

› Hot Lava helenium

HELENIUM 'HOT LAVA,' ZONES 3 TO 8

Hot Lava's non-drooping, outstretched petals provide an ever-changing display of color. The daisy-like flowers open yellow, develop orange and red streaks, and finally mature to red.

Why we love it: Dress up your indoor decor by adding these pretty, colorful blossoms to your fall bouquets.

JOE PYE: PERENNIALRESOURCE.COM; RUSSIAN SAGE: COURTESY OF PROVEN WINNERS - PROVENWINNERS.COM; HELENIUM: DOREENWYNJA.COM FOR MONROVIA

Waterlily crocus growing among Angelina sedum

^ Waterlily autumn crocus

COLCHICUM 'WATERLILY,' ZONES 4 TO 7

Add a colorful surprise to the front of your garden with the large leafless blooms of Waterlily autumn crocus. Plant the bulbs in late summer and then enjoy the flowers right away in fall. Next spring, 6-to-14-inch-tall leaves appear for about 8 weeks and then fade away for summer. Each fall, the flowers reappear, sans leaves.

Why we love it: Autumn crocus looks absolutely stunning among spring-flowering ground covers.

^ Mr. Goodbud sedum

SEDUM 'MR. GOODBUD,' ZONES 3 TO 9

There's a lot to love about this fall-blooming sedum. The red-tinged foliage and purple-red stems add color to your spring and summer garden. Autumn brings contrasting white buds that open into 5-to-6-inch clusters of vibrant purple-pink flowers.

Why we love it: The strong, purple-red stems keep the plant upright and prevent it from flopping over. Plus, sedum remains standing for winter interest.

‹ Hot Lips turtlehead

CHELONE LYONII 'HOT LIPS,' ZONES 3 TO 8

The vibrant rosy-pink color is sure to lure you in for a closer look at the uniquely shaped flowers. Dark green leaves and red stems add to its appeal. Grow this versatile plant in full sun to part shade.

Why we love it: The species is native to wet woodlands and streams, making it a great choice for those tricky moist areas and rain gardens.

WATERLILY: WHITEFLOWER FARM; SEDUM: JACKSON & PERKINS/TERRA NOVA NURSERIES; TURTLEHEAD: DOREENWYNJA.COM FOR MONROVIA

Unconventional Evergreens

Branch out beyond typical trees and shrubs with perennial plants that will add year-round color to your yard

By Wendy Helfenbaum

THE STANDARDS FOR UNWAVERING GREENERY are often conifers or broadleaf bushes, but there are countless opportunities to get creative with other evergreen plants. Not only do they feature pretty foliage year-round, but many also produce showy blooms or berries, provide winter interest and attract wildlife, says Lorin Nielsen, head horticulturist and senior botanical editor of *Epic Gardening* in San Diego, California.

"Some evergreens pick up reddish tinges in the fall, have variegated colors or get lighter in color during the peak summer heat," Lorin says. "The fruit or fallen seeds from the flowers provide food for birds. Low evergreen heath plants from the Ericaceae plant family bloom in the winter or spring, providing some of the first flowers that pollinators rely on for sustenance, and many perennial ground covers can shelter insects or small wildlife."

Early-blooming perennials also bridge the gap from winter through the arrival of the first annual flowers, and some evergreens are edible, Lorin adds.

"Creeping rosemary, a common woody ground cover plant, is a staple in my yard. Not only does it produce tiny blue flowers at multiple times of the year, but it also provides me with a never-ending supply of fresh rosemary for cooking," she says.

Fall is the ideal time for the southern half of the United States to plant evergreen perennials so the plant can stretch out its roots into your soil before winter. Or start from seed indoors in the winter and plant in late winter to early spring, Lorin suggests. In northern regions, plant evergreens in early spring as the weather warms.

"If you have a sudden burst of heat or a snap frost, protect your plant with shade cloth (for heat) or frost blankets (for cold)," she adds.

Before investing in an evergreen, check which species will overwinter best in your zone.

Mediterranean spurge

JOHN MARTIN/ALAMY STOCK PHOTO

^ Aureomaculata leopard plant

FARFUGIUM JAPONICUM, ZONES 7 TO 9

A member of the sunflower family, this herbaceous perennial has yellow blooms from summer through fall with 6-to-12-inch-long yellow-spotted dark green leaves on hairy reddish stems.

^ Lungwort

PULMONARIA, ZONES 3 TO 8

Speckled silvery green foliage adds interest while bees and hummingbirds enjoy the rich blue, purple and white flowers that blossom from salmon-pink buds in early spring.

‹ Mediterranean spurge

EUPHORBIA CHARACIAS, ZONES 6 TO 8

This sculptural plant features blue-green foliage with neon green bracts from February through May. It provides drama against a wall, in a large pot or in the back of your border.

› Black Scallop bugleweed

AJUGA REPTANS, ZONES 3 TO 10

This compact ground cover features glossy dark purple foliage and some tiny spikes of rich blue flowers for pollinators in mid- to late spring. It needs well-draining soil and can be invasive in some areas.

AUREOMACULATA: LITTLE PRINCE OF OREGON NURSERY WWW.LITTLEPRINCEPLANTS.COM; LUNGWORT: ANGHI, MEDITERRANEAN SPURGE: MICHAEL DERRER FUCHS/SHUTTERSTOCK (2);

^ Excalibur Adam's needle

YUCCA FILAMENTOSA, ZONES 4 TO 10

This cultivar of a native develops into a rounded, spiky clump that produces white bell-shaped blossoms in early summer while tolerating dry soil. Its spiky, blue- or gray-green foliage features curly white filaments.

› Fun and Games Capture the Flag foamy bells

HEUCHERELLA HYBRID, ZONES 4 TO 9

Bees flock to this large-leaved, mounded perennial's fluffy white flowers, which top chartreuse leaves with rich red centers. Plant it as a border or in containers in humus-rich, well-draining soil.

^ Fairytale Romance pigsqueak

BERGENIA, ZONES 4 TO 10

An early-spring bloomer with pink flowers, this perennial has glossy green foliage that turns reddish in cooler weather, making it a great ground cover or rock garden addition.

‹ Jerusalem sage

PHLOMIS RUSSELIANA, ZONES 5 TO 9

This hardy, drought-tolerant perennial produces creamy yellow hooded blooms in late spring that stay upright all winter for birds to nibble on. Olive-green heart-shaped foliage adds extra interest.

COMPANY; JERUSALEM SAGE: ALEX MANDERS//GETTY IMAGES

^ Marmalade coral bells

HEUCHERA, ZONES 4 TO 9

With its shiny ruffled foliage ranging from umber to red to orangey brown with pink undersides that change color, this vigorous variety becomes a compact mound.

^ Bowles' Mauve shrubby wallflower

ERISYIUM, ZONES 5 TO 10

This long-blooming, drought-tolerant variety attracts butterflies to its fragrant clusters of mauve flowers over gray-green foliage. Encourage autumn flowering by cutting it back to 6 inches in midsummer.

‹ Purple Beauty hens-and-chicks

SEMPERVIVUM, ZONES 3 TO 8

Ideal in rock gardens and walkway crevices, sempervivum's large rosette (the hen) and surrounding smaller rosettes (the chicks) are clusters of succulent leaves in shades of rich purple with green centers. To divide, pull up some chicks and replant elsewhere.

› Husker Red beardtongue

PENSTEMON, ZONES 4 TO 9

Featuring striking deep green foliage with maroon undersides, this native variety produces dainty white flowers in the summer, attracting hummingbirds and butterflies. Birds gobble up the seeds in cooler months.

CORAL BELLS: ANNA GRATYS, WALLFLOWER: RUKIMEDIA/SHUTTERSTOCK (2); PURPLE BEAUTY: LITTLE PRINCE OF OREGON NURSERY WWW.LITTLEPRINCEPLANTS.COM; BEARDTONGUE: SUSAN HODGSON/SHUTTERSTOCK

^ Chinese fringe flower

LOROPETALUM, ZONES 7 TO 9

This easy-to-grow member of the witch hazel family features green, purple or burgundy foliage. Butterflies love the vibrant pink, red, cream or white flowers that bloom from midwinter to early spring.

^ Snowsation evergreen candytuft

IBERIS SEMPERVIRENS, ZONES 3 TO 8

This drought-tolerant pick draws butterflies with its flurry of large white flowers that appear in mid- to late spring over a compact mound of foliage. Try it as edging or in rock gardens.

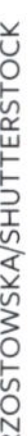
BRZOSTOWSKA/SHUTTERSTOCK

Favorite Evergreens

Lorin Nielsen, head horticulturist and senior botanical editor of *Epic Gardening* in San Diego, shares some of her top picks and what makes them special.

Winter heath

Winter heath: "I'm a huge fan of winter heath plants! Saskia winter heath has rose-pink flowers throughout winter, and Whitehall winter heath has snow white flowers."

Lingonberry

Lingonberry: For edible gardening in Zones 8 and colder, Lorin suggests trying lingonberry: "It produces tiny bell-shaped flowers in the spring and edible berries later in the year."

Evergreen candytuft

Evergreen candytuft: "It thrives in sun and part shade, and when growing under the canopy of larger trees, it produces lovely linear-leaved green foliage throughout the year. In spring, their racemes, crammed with white flowers, breathe life into your winter-ravaged landscape."

Beeblossom

Beeblossom: For stunning curb appeal, consider the dwarf cultivar, Belleza Compact Light Pink beeblossom. It has small green leaves at the base from which tall reddish flower stalks rise with vibrant pink or white star-shaped flowers. "These are perfect in a cottage garden," says Lorin. "And during winter, they create a pleasant green mound of foliage."

Fall Gardening

Our readers give the lowdown on how they keep their backyard blooming in autumn

Bittersweet

Autumn Allure

Even when summer is fading, plenty of flowers and plants thrive as the mercury dips. Give these a try.

- Anemone
- Aster
- Balloon flower
- Bittersweet
- Black-eyed Susan
- Chrysanthemum
- Coreopsis
- Firethorn
- Goldenrod
- Joe Pye weed
- Lobelia
- Nasturtium
- Pansy
- Phlox
- Rose
- Russian sage
- Sedum
- Sunflower
- Virginia creeper

Chrysanthemums

TERRY WILD/TERRY WILD STOCK (2)

The secret to compact and beautiful chrysanthemums is to pinch back or trim about half of the plant's new growth. Repeat this until about the first week of July. And be sure to water and fertilize properly.

Leroy Martin
HAGERSTOWN, MD

I like to plant assorted varieties of sedum in pots. They survive winter in our area and do well even if the containers get dry in summer. It's a great, versatile plant.

Valerie Giesbrecht
OTHELLO, WA

This perennial garden has great foliage and texture, which will transition nicely into fall.

Here at our house, we use flower beds year-round. We have raised brick beds leading up to our front door, and it's a great place to show off the season's best colors.

This is an easy project anyone can do. No matter what size your flower beds are, there's something for every season. We plant mums in fall, cabbage in winter, tulips in spring and then various annuals in summer. So don't call it quits for the year just yet. There's plenty of gardening left to do!

Kenneth Welty
SPRINGFIELD, VA

A few years ago, my husband and son built raised beds for my perennials. I really wanted to see my plants bloom in succession and have vibrant color all season long, so I planned my garden to include plants with many different bloom times.

My perennials include lilies, beardtongue, liatris, coneflower, blanket flower, phlox, coreopsis, lavender, Shasta daisies and a few others.

After the perennials fade, my annuals steal the show. I planted petunias, zinnias, gladioluses, calla lilies, poppies, nasturtium, bachelor's buttons and celosia.

I love watching the flowers come up, open and shine in a succession of blooms!

Nancy Smith
JOHNSTON CITY, IL

TERRY WILD/TERRY WILD STOCK (2)

I plant a late tomato crop in early August along with lots of zinnias, cosmos, marigolds and pansies. They love the cooler weather.

Ginny Taney Harnsberger
VIA FACEBOOK

I carefully dig up my favorite geraniums and bring them indoors. I put them in a sunny window and they bloom all winter!

Tina Eitemiller
VIA FACEBOOK

In autumn, when the plants in my flower box are done blooming, I fill it with dried flowers from my garden. This way I can enjoy its beauty all year round.

Victoria Tesch WAUSAU, WI

Want your petunias to last throughout summer? Try my easy approach. Cut back petunias in mid-July. This is good for two reasons: It keeps them short and bushy, and it also helps them bloom longer.

Mary Stager SILVER MAY, MN

To keep a garden in bloom for a long time, alternate your rows with flowers that bloom at different times. One good combination is dahlias, gladioluses and zinnias.

Liz McCain FLORENCE, OR

Want your hanging fuchsia basket to keep blooming? Just pinch off the spent flowers. Do this constantly, and the plant will bloom all summer.

Margaret Lindow
SUAMICO, WI

In mild winter areas, it's easy to grow new rosebushes from your existing plants.

Here are a few tips to keep your roses beautiful throughout the growing season.

- In early spring, trim back the dead canes. Then fertilize the plants with granular rose food, working it lightly into the soil.
- Each month throughout the summer, fertilize using a balanced rose food.
- Make sure roses are well watered. To get the most out of each watering and to protect them from disease, water only at the base of the plant.
- To keep your roses blooming throughout the growing season, trim off spent blooms.
- In more northerly areas, prune back your roses to allow for winter protection. Don't prune too much, though. Your main pruning should be done in spring.
- The winters in your area will typically determine how you should mound or cover your roses to protect them until spring. When in doubt, it doesn't hurt to add a little extra cover.

Jeanette Dalton
MOUNTAIN GROVE, MO

If you live in an area with mild winters, it's easy to start new rosebushes from your existing ones. Whenever you prune them, just use the cuttings to root new plants.

You can dip the tips of the cuttings into rooting hormone first, but I've had success just planting them right in the soil. With this easy method, my garden is always filled with beautiful roses.

Julie Soileau MARBURY, AL

Rosebush blooms don't have to be short-lived. After a rosebush blooms and the flowers fade, I cut the flowering stems down to the next leaf with five leaflets. The plant often continues to bloom into late summer and sometimes early fall.

Jan Grage CENTERVILLE, SD

GARDEN: TERRY WILD/TERRY WILD STOCK; ROSE: BILL JOHNSON

When you trim your chrysanthemums back in summer, you may be able to enjoy even more flowers later. I plant the tops I've cut off in the soil along our garage wall. Soon I have enough new plants to share with friends and neighbors.

Martha Miller AUBURN HILLS, MI

I wait to plant my sunflowers until June 1. They will grow well into fall and even survive a few cold nights.

Shelley Seldman VIA FACEBOOK

Sunflowers carry over nicely into fall.

Here's a hint for keeping a new perennial bed vibrant all summer long: Interplant it with colorful annuals. The annuals will fill in the bare spots until your perennials get established. If your perennial yard is in its second or third year, plant the annuals in pots and add them wherever you'd like color.

Marie Blahut YORKTON, SK

Rejuvenate old perennials by dividing them. If the center of the plant is woody and no longer produces flowers, divide it in half. Cut out and discard the center and cut the remaining ring into smaller pieces. Plant some of these pieces in the same spot, and soon you'll see new growth. Plant extra pieces in other areas, or share them with friends.

Angela Griffin Hatchett
ALTOONA, AL

Time for a Trim

10 perennials you can cut back every fall (and five to leave alone)

By Lisa Meyers McClintick

IN THE CRUNCH OF THE ANNUAL fall cleanup, remember to make time for perennial care too.

Cutting back foliage protects flowering plants from disease and provides a clean start for regrowth. But many perennial plants are worth leaving up if they're healthy, since letting them stand for winter can increase their hardiness and benefit wildlife.

Dick Zondag, former president of Wisconsin-based J.W. Jung Seed Co., offers tips for getting perennials ready, if you choose to trim them. So grab a pruner and start cropping these 10 plants.

1. Iris

This showy summer favorite is vulnerable to infestations of iris borers, which tunnel into the base of the rhizome to lay eggs. Trim the fan of sword-shaped leaves at an angle so they slope upward into a center peak no higher than 6 to 8 inches. Then remove any dead or dried leaf debris.

2. Bee Balm

Cutting back this plant keeps it healthy for the hummingbirds and butterflies that flock to it in midsummer. Bring it down to the soil to discourage problems such as mildew. If plants show signs of mildew, dispose of the cuttings instead of composting them.

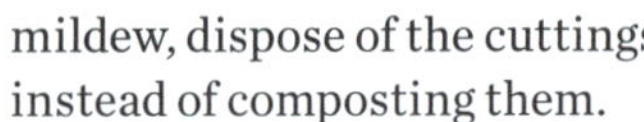

3. Peony

Gorgeous peonies are also vulnerable to mildew. Grab the leaves and prune the stems to a few inches after the first frost.

4. Daylily

Clip back the profusion of daylily leaves that burst from rhizomes like fireworks. If desired, reach down near the base of each plant to secure a tight handful of leaves and cut.

5. Lily

Dick suggests paying attention to

1: LOUIS PUTTKAY; 2, 3, 6, 9: CONEFLOWER; COURTESY OF PROVEN WINNERS - WWW.PROVENWINNERS.COM (5); 4: PATRICIA GLYNN; 5: KELLY FRISINA-BLAND; 7: SUSAN WORSHAM; 8: KOICHI WATANABE/GETTY IMAGES; 10: RICHARD NIMTZ

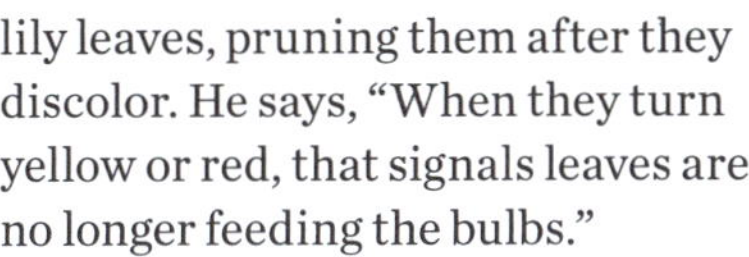

lily leaves, pruning them after they discolor. He says, "When they turn yellow or red, that signals leaves are no longer feeding the bulbs."

It only takes one quick snip of the stalk near the soil line, and you're done. Sometimes the stalk comes off with a gentle twist.

6. Phlox

Like bee balm, this super fragrant flower likes to spread and can be vulnerable to mildew. Take it down to the soil during fall to help prevent this disease.

7. Blazing Star

This plant's bright purple flowering spikes often appear in butterfly gardens. Trim flower spikes and leaves to the base so it's ready for another year of bold, striking color and texture.

8. Chrysanthemum

This fall star's flowers can be cut back after they've bloomed or been hit by a hard frost. Pair with leaves or other mulch, which can insulate the plant from harmful freeze-and-thaw cycles.

9. Hosta

Prune hosta leaves near the crown to keep the shade-loving perennial healthy. Keeping hostas neat and tidy reduces the risk of slugs taking over and harming the plants once spring returns.

10. Hollyhock

A cottage-garden staple, hollyhocks can get pretty gangly in the fall. Bring them down to about 6 inches high to reduce the risk of leaf rust. If you have seedpods, scatter them in fall for more plants come spring.

Still Standing

Leave these five plants upright in colder months.

- Coneflowers
- Hibiscus
- Ornamental grasses
- Russian sage
- Sedums

White coneflowers in a container

At-Home Harvest

A step-by-step guide to growing the best backyard pumpkins and gourds

By Niki Jabbour

W**HETHER DRESSING UP INDOOR AND OUTDOOR** spaces in fall or starring in seasonal desserts, pumpkins and gourds are autumn musts. To harvest them from your own garden next year, follow these simple tips to get a head start on your personal patch.

Pumpkins and gourds are members of the Cucurbitaceae family. When growing your own, pick from the wide assortment available in seed catalogs or online. Certain pumpkins are best for carving, while others make the sweetest pies. Read carefully to select pumpkins that meet your garden goals. Fruit sizes range from mini to massive; colors include classic orange as well as white, red, green, blue and yellow; and shapes vary from flat to round to tall.

Gourds are also rewarding to grow. Two main types of gourds are available to gardeners: hard-shell and ornamental. Hard-shell gourds, such as birdhouse or long-dipper gourds, can be dried and kept indefinitely. The fruits are also edible when harvested immature. Ornamental gourds produce unique fruits in a wide mix of shapes, sizes and colors, but they aren't edible and don't dry well, so they're best used as decor in autumn and then added to the compost pile.

Taking Care

Once in the garden, pumpkins and gourds are easygoing. Keep an eye on soil moisture, watering deeply when the soil is dry. Water the soil, not the plant, as splashing water can increase the risk of soil-borne disease. Promote healthy growth by fertilizing every two to three weeks with either a liquid kelp or a fish fertilizer.

Also watch out for pests such as squash bugs and squash vine borers. If borers are an annual issue in your garden, wrap a 6-inch piece of aluminum foil around the bottom of each stem. This helps reduce the number of female vine borers laying eggs on the plant stems.

When several pumpkins have formed on each vine, remember to pinch back the growing tip. This directs the plant's energy into maturing existing fruits, not producing more flowers. The late flowers won't have time to mature into good-sized pumpkins. Pinching also leads to bigger pumpkins. Pinching hard-shell gourds is helpful too, but there's no need to prune back the plants of ornamental gourds.

During summer, another task to consider is pollination. Gourds and pumpkins produce separate male and female flowers. Pollen needs to be transferred from a male flower to a female flower for fruits to form. Bees typically take care of this, but you can lend Mother Nature a hand by using a small clean paintbrush to move pollen to the flowers. Hand pollinate on a dry, sunny day.

Perfect Planting

Though they are pretty easy to grow, success with pumpkins and gourds begins with selecting the right spot. They need at least eight hours of sun each day as well as room for the vines to roam. If you lack growing space, plant bush or semi-bush options that don't produce long vines.

Pumpkins and gourds are greedy plants, growing best when the soil is enhanced with several inches of compost or aged manure. It's also a good idea to apply a slow-release organic vegetable fertilizer to the garden bed before planting them.

The heat-loving fruits shouldn't be rushed into the spring garden since the seeds don't germinate well in cold soil. Wait it out until your area's last frost date has passed and the soil has warmed to 70 degrees. Then direct sow or transplant seeds into raised beds, in-ground gardens, straw bales or hills, which are small mounds of soil piled up to improve drainage and raise soil temperature. Sow seeds a half inch to an inch deep. Spacing depends on the selected variety. Refer to your seed packets for specific spacing information.

Proper Timing

Consider the length of your growing season—most pumpkin and gourd varieties need 90 to 125 days to mature. Read seed packets carefully and pick varieties that have time to grow in your region.

Time to Harvest

First-time growers may have a hard time knowing when it's time to harvest their pumpkins and gourds. The biggest clue is the fruit's color. With a sharp pair of pruners, clip fruits from vines when they've turned their mature color. Leave a 2-to-4-inch-long stem attached to each fruit. Be sure to harvest before a hard frost, which can damage the fruits.

Let pumpkins and gourds cure in the sun for five to seven days if the weather allows. Curing keeps pumpkins from decaying too quickly. If cold and frost are threats, bring the fruits indoors to a warm spot with decent air circulation to cure.

PREVIOUS SPREAD: EYEWOLF/GETTY IMAGES; THIS SPREAD, LEFT: PLG PHOTO/SHUTTERSTOCK; RIGHT: SHIVER PUMPKIN: PHOTO BY JOHNNYSEEDS.COM; BLUE PRINCE: ALL-AMERICA SELECTIONS;

Toad pumpkin

Blue Prince pumpkin

Silver Edged pumpkin

Blanco pumpkin

Patch Perfect

Six pumpkin varieties to try.

Toad
This compact plant, perfect for small gardens or containers, produces five to six small bright orange pumpkins covered with large bumps.

Blue Prince
These large flattened blue-gray pumpkins are both decorative and delicious. Use the roasted creamy flesh in your favorite hearty and homey fall recipes.

Silver Edged
The vine yields a heavy crop of green and silvery white striped fruits. The 5-to-8-pound fleshy pumpkins are packed with large seeds for roasting.

Shiver
Compact pumpkins with ghostly white skin and a round shape grow on a bush-type plant ideal for small spaces.

Blanco
The smooth white pumpkins are deer resistant and just the right size for small jack-o'-lanterns.

Lemonade
Golden yellow skin adds a new hue to autumn decor.

Shiver pumpkin

Lemonade pumpkin

Embrace Autumn Colors

This season brings new opportunities for rich colors and fall interest with these pretty plant picks and creative combos

By Kaitlin Stainbrook

Graceful Grasses Vertigo Purple fountain grass

1 Superbells Pomegranate Punch calibrachoa

COURTESY OF PROVEN WINNERS - WWW.PROVENWINNERS.COM (2)

3
Supertunia
Honey petunia
4
Superbells
Tropical Sunrise
calibrachoa
2
Graceful Grasses
Fireworks
fountain grass

Coordinating Your Containers

When combining plants, try selecting a trio that can fulfill each of these roles.

THRILLER: Strong colors or heavy visual interest; typically centered in container.

FILLER: Rounded growth that fills container space, making it look full.

SPILLER: Trailing growth typically placed at edge of container to hang over side.

Sunsatia Blood Orange

Superbells Red

^ Cape Jewels

Also known as nemesia, cape jewels are native to South Africa. These flowers are typically grown as annuals. Cape jewels tend to perform best in well-draining containers, and they come in a wide variety of colors. "Their snapdragon-like flowers are fragrant, and they can tolerate light frosts," says Allen Pyle, a horticulture expert at University of Wisconsin, Madison's Division of Extension.

Variety to try: Sunsatia Blood Orange is low maintenance, thanks to being self-cleaning, meaning that instead of needing deadheading, the spent blooms will blow away in the wind.

^ Calibrachoa

If you're looking for continuous blooms that cascade over the sides of hanging baskets and containers, look no further than calibrachoa. Being sensitive to both high and low pH levels, they do best with regular doses of a well-balanced fertilizer. Although it's not necessary, you can give them a trim to increase branching and create fuller plants.

Variety to try: Bring in the hummingbirds with their favorite color. Superbells Red boasts pure red blooms that continue to look great into fall.

Tuscan Sun

‹ False Sunflower

False sunflower, or oxeye sunflower, may look like a true sunflower at first glance, but it's a powerful perennial for containers thanks to its shorter height (3 to 5 feet) and golden blooms that continue to shine past summer. It's relatively hardy and can even handle dry, rocky soil.

Variety to try: You can skip the staking with Tuscan Sun false sunflower. This plant is incredibly compact and is an eye-catching choice for the "thriller" in a mixed container. Plus, bees and butterflies love it!

Superbena Royale Plum Wine

^ Common Verbena

"Typically grown as an annual, common verbena is actually a tender perennial in mild winter climates," says Allen. It's an extremely long bloomer (spring to early frost), but make sure to plant it in a space that receives full sun. "Verbena's abundant flowers attract pollinators, including butterflies and hummingbirds," Allen adds. **Variety to try:** Superbena Royale Plum Wine pulls double duty as either "filler" or "spiller" in a mixed container, thanks to its mounded shape and trailing growth. Plant verbena in a smaller container for best results.

Bright Lights White

^ African Daisy

Although several species go by the common name African daisy, look for *Osteospermum*—plants within this genus are more cold tolerant and work best in fall containers. "African daisy produces attractive flowers that bloom more heavily in cooler conditions, such as spring and fall," Allen says. **Variety to try:** For big blooms that do well in cooler fall temps but are also heat tolerant, consider Bright Lights White African daisy. This variety isn't a fan of heavy watering, though, so allow the top soil to dry out before grabbing your watering can.

› Coral Bells

This perennial proves foliage can be the colorful star of the show too. "Foliage color in coral bells ranges from bronze to red-purple, purple, peach shades, green with silver highlights—and many more," Allen says. "*Heuchera*, or coral bells, are an excellent choice for adding texture to mixed containers, and their flowers attract hummingbirds." **Variety to try:** Primo Black Pearl has dark ruffled leaves that make a dramatic statement. As with other coral bell varieties, you should move it to your landscape in early fall if you want it to reappear next year.

Primo Black Pearl

Choosing the Right Size

Allen suggests not holding back when it comes to container size. "Generally for containers, the bigger the better—as long as the filled containers are not too large and heavy to move when needed," he says. "Large containers hold more nutrients and water, requiring less frequent watering and fertilization than smaller containers do."

Invest in Next Spring

Plant these bulbs in fall for carpets of color the following year

By Eva Monheim

ACONITE: ROMAOSLO, CAMAS: KEVIN SCHAFER, TROUT LILY: JACKY PARKER PHOTOGRAPHY/GETTY IMAGES (3); SIBERIAN SQUILL: IAN TALBOYS/ALAMY STOCK PHOTO

‹ Winter aconite

ERANTHIS HYEMALIS, ZONES 4 TO 7

Tough and resilient, winter aconites provide brilliant yellow morsels of joy in the garden as they begin to awaken around March in many areas. The tubers multiply over time, providing even more brilliant color. The low, buttercuplike flower's frilly green collar accents the yellow petals. Full to part sun is ideal.

Why we love it: This low-growing plant shines along pathways, is exceptionally deer resistant and can even grow under black walnut trees.

^ Camas

CAMASSIA LEICHTLINII SSP. *SUKSDORFII*, ZONES 5 TO 9

Lovely stalks of blue-purple star-shaped flowers grow up to 4 feet tall and bloom from April to May. Camas plants tolerate a range of soils from clay to wet or dry ground, and work well in rain gardens. The flowers come in an array of colors, including white, purple, blue and cream. The yellow anthers make the flower petals pop.

Why we love it: Camas is native to the western U.S., and bees appreciate the pollen in late spring.

^ Pagoda trout lily

ERYTHRONIUM CALIFORNICUM, ZONES 3 TO 9

Pagoda is one of the largest trout lilies, standing up to a foot tall. With sulfur yellow flowers, it brightens partly shaded gardens, and deer and rabbits leave it alone. This lily goes dormant after blooming, so plant it among perennials that start to shine in early summer.

Why we love it: In addition to the bright flowers, the plant's leaves are a glossy green, sporting bronze and maroon markings that fade later in the season.

‹ Siberian squill

SCILLA SIBERICA, ZONES 2 TO 8

Small clusters of brilliant blue flowers grow on stems accompanied by long, slender and strappy leaves. Their nodding heads look like a wave across the garden during a spring breeze. Do not plant Siberian squill in the Great Lakes region or the Northeast, where it's invasive.

Why we love it: Siberian squill looks fantastic clustered around a tree and is hardy in very cold areas.

^ Persian lily

FRITILLARIA PERSICA, ZONES 4 TO 8

From mid- to late spring, Persian lily puts on quite a show with its flowers, which range from deep purple to cream. The flowers can tower over the garden, maxing out at 3 feet tall. They prefer well-draining soil and full sun to part shade. Each stalk holds dozens of blossoms. It's an excellent cut flower, adding drama to bouquets.

Why we love it: Persian lily adapts to varying soils, as long as they're well-draining.

^ Gravetye Giant summer snowflake

LEUCOJUM AESTIVUM, ZONES 4 TO 8

Growing a little over 2 feet tall once they're established, Gravetye Giant features deep green, grasslike leaves and white, bell-shaped flowers with a green marking on the tip of each petal. It naturalizes in full sun or part shade, and the flowers smell slightly like chocolate.

Why we love it: You can plant it in a range of soils, including clay. The bulbs are resistant to disease in well-draining soil.

› Glory of the snow

CHIONODOXA LUCILIAE, ZONES 3 TO 8

This diminutive plant stands 4 to 6 inches tall with blooms in purple, blue or sometimes pink with a white center. It covers the ground from March to April, depending on your location, and does well in snow. The plants fade quickly after the initial bloom but come back year after year with the right care.

Why we love it: Glory of the snow grows under black walnut trees, deer don't seem to care for it, and it makes lovely small flower arrangements in early spring.

^ Spring starflower

IPHEION SPECIES, ZONES 5 TO 9

The shape of the blooms is the best way to identify this plant, also known as springstar. The flowers exude a spicy fragrance, and the leaves smell like garlic when crushed. Stems grow 6 inches tall in full sun and tolerate some shade. They look right at home in rock and woodland gardens.

Why we love it: Bees and other early pollinators are attracted to the plant.

^ Spanish bluebell

HYACINTHOIDES HISPANICA, ZONES 3 TO 8

Spanish bluebell varieties come in shades of blue, pink and white with deep green foliage accentuating the 1-to-2-foot-tall flower stalks. Plant bulbs in part sun to part shade for the best results, but it also grows in full sun or full shade.

Why we love it: Pollinators can't get enough of it, and it's a fantastic transitional bulb to bridge late spring and summer.

< Windflower

ANEMONE BLANDA, ZONES 5 TO 8

Windflowers are an excellent ground cover, and they can be found in blue-purple, white and pink varieties. The lobed leaves add beautiful textured interest. You can also plant the tubers, mixed with other bulbs and perennials, in pots.

Why we love it: This plant features charming 8-inch-tall daisylike flowers and is disease and pest resistant.

STOCK PHOTO; BLUEBELL: JACKY PARKER PHOTOGRAPHY/GETTY IMAGES; WINDFLOWER: SWAPAN PHOTOGRAPHY/SHUTTERSTOCK

Garden Under Cover

From traditional methods to creative ingenuity, follow these handy tips to extend the growing season beyond the first frost.

By Melinda Myers

A cold frame with a clear top lets sunlight in.

Winter growing setups can range from complex, like these strawberries in a high tunnel, to one tomato plant in a simple milk carton.

FROM LEFT: JUDYWHITE/GARDENPHOTOS.COM; BARMALINI/SHUTTERSTOCK

Make a cloche from a 2-liter bottle. Cut the bottom off the bottle and place it around precious plants for cold-weather protection.

CELEBRATE THE CHANGING SEASONS by harvesting veggies and planting new seeds even when the ground is frozen. Use these methods to keep your garden going through the cold or start growing earlier next spring, regardless of your location.

Build a Tiny Greenhouse

Gardeners have used cloches for centuries to protect small plants from treacherous weather—think of them as miniature, portable greenhouses. Originally they were large, clear bell-shaped jars. Glass cloches are still available, but most gardeners find plastic and fabric varieties more affordable and easier to use. Many have built-in vents, which eliminate the need to remove or tilt the cloche for hot air to escape.

If you're crafty—and even if you're not—you can make your own tiny greenhouse. It's easy; just cut off the bottom of a gallon milk jug and place the DIY cloche over transplants in spring or smaller plants, such as herbs, in fall. Remove the cap on sunny days, but be sure to put it back on chilly nights.

Use a Frame

Cold frames are another traditional favorite. They capture the sun's heat and light through a clear material covering, forming a warm, humid environment for plants. The structure provides ample space to start seeds, acclimate transplants to the outdoors, and extend your garden and harvest seasons. At one time, they were made of wood and covered with clear glass. Today you can find them in an array of materials such as cedar, aluminum and plastic.

Or leave store-bought types behind and build your own cold frame. Use old windows, shower doors or other transparent items for the top. While most cold frames are 3 to 4 feet deep and 4 to 8 feet long, you might need to adjust those dimensions based on the top piece you've picked. The back of the cold frame is usually taller than the front wall, 18 to 30 inches versus 12 to 24 inches, creating an angled roof to catch

What's in a Frame?

Harvest these plants all winter long.

CHARD: BONCHAN. CARROTS: NATTIKA. BEETS: VALENTINA RAZUMOVA/SHUTTERSTOCK (3); ONIONS, KALE, SCALLIONS: STOCKBYTE/PUNCHSTOCK (3); SPINACH: OPTIMARC/SHUTTERSTOCK

more light. If possible, set your cold frame in a sheltered location for added insulation, and position the front facing south to absorb the most light and heat.

You'll need to pay attention to the conditions inside the frame whether it was manufactured or homemade. Cover the top with old carpets, straw or other warmth-preserving items on cold nights, and partially open the lid to ventilate on sunny days when temperatures get too steamy for the plants. A commercially available temperature-sensitive cold frame ventilator also does the job.

Keep Them Covered

If you like the idea of a cold frame but need more space for larger, mature plants, try a high tunnel. This season-extender is similar to a cold frame but taller. It uses hoops made of plastic or metal, covered with a layer of sheet plastic, to create a plant-friendly environment.

Row covers may be the ideal option for the construction-averse. The multifaceted fabrics allow water and light through the material while trapping plant-saving heat, and they also shroud plants, creating a protective barrier from the elements. Check the product's temperature rating, and buy the one that is best suited to your climate.

To use, just drape the fabric over plants, allowing enough slack for them to grow. Anchor the sides of the fabric with boards, stones, pipes or landscape pins. There's no need to ventilate; just lift it to harvest or when the temperatures are suitable for growing.

Sow Summer Seeds

Winter sowing allows you to start seeds of your favorite perennials, annual flowers, vegetables or herbs in potting mix and milk jugs outdoors, months before the ground thaws. To get going, partially cut a milk jug about 3 to 4 inches from the bottom to create a hinged top. Then punch four holes in the bottom of the container and fill it with quality potting mix. Gently add water to settle the potting mix, and plant the seeds at the recommended depth.

Label what's inside and seal the contraption with duct tape. Remove the cap and place the jug in a sunny location where rain and snow will reach it. Start hardy perennials any time during the winter, and begin growing other plants one or two months before you would normally sow outdoor seedings.

With a variety of simple methods to choose from and benefits aplenty, it's easy to keep your garden green and growing between the first and last frosts.

Winter Garden Gear

Top picks to keep your garden going in winter.

Keep seedlings protected with **Red Tomato Teepees.** They use pockets of water to insulate and warm the soil for garden favorites such as tomatoes, peppers and other transplants, providing a jump of up to six weeks on the planting and harvest seasons. Available at *gardeners.com.*

The **Row Garden Cloche** is more than 3 feet long and features a built-in adjustable vent that allows you to control the internal temperature. Use the handle to lift the cover and harvest with ease. Available at *gardeners.com.*

The **Fleece Tunnel** protects 10 feet of crops from harsh weather, pesky insects and wildlife. Wire hoops are sewn directly into the cover, which closes at each end with a drawstring. Available at *territorialseed.com.*

TOMATO TEEPEES, GARDEN CLOCHE: PHOTO COURTESY OF GARDENER'S SUPPLY COMPANY (2); FLEECE TUNNEL: TERRITORIAL SEED COMPANY

8 Garden Chores You Can't Ignore

Even if time is tight, focus on these fall cleanup tasks that fellow gardeners say you should always finish before colder weather arrives

By Rachel Maidl

Clean and organized gardening tools

1

1: A. HART/GETTY IMAGES

2

Dig up nonhardy bulbs like dahlias for winter storage.

2: ELISE MARKS

WHEN IT COMES TO FALL CLEANUP, the work can add up. Judy Roberts of Graytown, Ohio, even jokes, "My list includes emptying pots and storing them, digging up calla lily tubers and removing all my ceramic garden decor. Phew—I'm tired just thinking about it!"

But, some of the fall cleanup chores are more important than others to keep your yard and gardens looking fantastic. They also set you up for success through winter and spring. Here are the tasks that *Birds & Blooms* readers never skip, no matter how busy they are.

1. Take Care of Garden Tools

It's possible for plants to swap diseases and parasites, but there are a few things you can do to help keep your plants healthy. One can't-skip autumn activity is cleaning and sharpening garden tools.

"I'm sure to clean all my garden utensils thoroughly," comments Joan Heid of Chester, South Carolina. She adds that it's also a great time to organize them, saying that she always "stores tools away for easy access in spring." Wipe tools clean of any sap, soil or dirt. If you've used a tool on a diseased plant, be sure to soak it in a 10% bleach solution and rinse it well with clear water. Allow the tool to dry thoroughly before storing it away to avoid rust. Also, replace any worn-out or damaged tools.

2. Dig Up Nonhardy Bulbs

Fall is the time to get down and dirty. Some plants grow well outdoors in the summer, but they just can't take the winter cold. Nonhardy bulbs like dahlias need to be dug up and stored for winter and then replanted in spring.

Lifting plants generally involves digging them up carefully, ridding them of excess dirt, allowing the bulb or tuber to dry out, and storing carefully in a cool dry place for the winter (garages are

often ideal, but protect your treasures from mice).

"I make sure to dig up the amaryllis bulb that I planted in spring and place it in a bag in a dark area to grow it again later," says Holly Ferkett of Pittsburgh, Pennsylvania.

3. Mulch Fall Leaves

Mulch can hold moisture in the ground (so you can water plants less often!) and even improve the soil quality.

Fallen leaves make excellent mulch for your lawn. So don't bag them up and throw them away. Lisa Malmberg of Green Bay, Wisconsin, says, "After gardening organically for over 30 years, I mulch all our beds with shredded leaves each autumn."

To do this fall cleanup chore yourself, just run a pile of leaves over with a lawn mower. The leaf mulch will be ready when the leaves are in quarter-sized pieces.

Lisa points out other benefits too. She says, "It's great for the plants and soil, and birds love all the insects they find in the leaves."

4. Turn Over the Soil

It's a hard job, but Pam Soetaert of Lampe, Missouri, says, "I always turn the garden soil over in the fall, because I'm six months younger than I will be the following spring!"

5. Create Brush and Yard Debris Piles

Piles of branches, sticks and other yard debris can be worth their weight in garden gold. These organic garden piles can be used as compost, broken down into mulch or serve as a home to helpful backyard bugs.

Greg Mandigo of Alma Center, Wisconsin, says, "Along with disease- and insect-free garden debris, I make a pile of leaves in my backyard. In spring, I use this mulch to cover potatoes and put around my plants."

6. Store Garden Hoses

Drain your garden hoses and bring them in when you're done, since water left in hoses over winter can lead to cracking and bursting.

7. Protect Your Roses

If you're a rose gardener, this is one of those fall cleanup garden chores that goes without saying. But if you're new to growing roses, or have a

3: ARIEL SKELLEY, 5: SANGHWAN KIM/GETTY IMAGES (2)

Natural mulch made with wood chips and leaves

special rose bush you'd like to protect, this chore is worth a few minutes of your time. Trim tall canes and cover roses with straw or evergreen boughs to protect the plants from cold weather.

If you use rose cones, make sure they are vented. You can also cover roses with dry leaves and wrap them with hardware cloth or burlap. Before covering your roses, make sure to clean up any diseased leaf debris and apply a new layer of mulch to your beds.

8. Mark Plant Locations

Now's the time to use sturdy plant markers to note the location of any new perennials, bulbs or seeds you might forget about come spring. There's probably nothing more frustrating than accidentally weeding out seedlings in the spring along with pesky weeds, or planting something on top of something else without realizing it. Labeling now saves you time and guesswork later.

There's no need for anything fancy. Try a permanent marker and paint stir stick, topped with a coat of clear gloss spray enamel. You surely don't need it to look pretty. You just need it to last until spring. The best part? It's fast, simple and super effective.

Trim tall canes and cover roses with straw or evergreen boughs to guard against the cold.

7: YVONNE GRANT

Backyard Cleanup

Gardeners reveal their top tips for tackling fall yard care and keeping things tidy before winter sets in

As long as your plants didn't have any problems this year, you can clean them out and add to your compost pile.

Every fall, I put my garden to bed by raking all my leaves into it. It's easy and helps the soil.

Ann Proffit BELLBROOK, OH

Don't pull out the dead annuals in your garden in fall. They'll come out much more easily in spring after the roots have rotted. If you cover your beds with leaves in fall, the annuals also help hold the leaves in place.

Jodie Stevenson
EXPORT, PA

Putting my garden to bed for the winter is a process that actually starts in midsummer. When annuals fade, I remove them and mulch the beds for winter. By late October, I've emptied the pots on my patio and cut back the few remaining perennials. When you make cleanup a continuous process, it isn't so overwhelming.

Marcia Briggs PITTSBURGH, PA

At the end of the season, I disinfect all my tools and tomato cages with a solution of 1 part bleach to 9 parts water. This can also be used during the growing season when handling diseased plants.

Sue Gronholz COLUMBUS, WI

In fall, we take all the garden extras (vegetables, stalks, vines, etc.) and drag them to the compost pile. Then we till the garden well. In spring, we just add composted horse manure and our gardens are ready to go.

Martha Odell
SIDNEY CENTER, NY

TERRY WILD/TERRY WILD STOCK (2)

Chrysanthemums

For a few years now, gardeners in my area have been holding perennial parties. Each spring and fall, different gardeners take turns hosting the gathering in their backyards. It's a great time to exchange tips, advice and plants. Roughly 150 gardeners are involved. We organize the plants by light needs and by type, such as herbs, daylilies and hostas. We have thousands of plants! A few of the ladies involved are master gardeners. They answer questions before the trading begins. Then we take turns picking plants until they're all gone. I've filled entire flower beds with these free plants, such as mums. I look forward to the event every autumn. I hope others can use this idea to start their own perennial parties.

Connie Baumann
LINO LAKES, MN

Don't spend a lot of money to create a new flower bed. Cover the area with old carpet in fall. By spring, the grass will be dead, and the soil will be moist and ready to till.

Barb Wagner WILLMAR, MN

Every summer, I take photos of my garden. In fall, I mount them in a lined notebook and write comments under each photo. I record what I planted that year, plants I'd like to try and tips to improve next year's garden. It's a big help to write these things down when they're fresh in my mind. Then for spring, I'm ready.

Karen Andrews
PETERSBURG, ON

To clean rusty garden tools, I rub them with a steel-wool soap pad dipped in turpentine. Then I polish them with wadded aluminum foil. I love the results!

Mary Ohms CARROLLTON, TX

It's good to leave up some plants into fall and winter because they'll make a good food source for birds.

TERRY WILD/TERRY WILD STOCK (2)

After raking autumn leaves into bags, I pile the bags in an out-of-the-way corner. In spring, I line the aisles of the garden with old newspaper and cover it with the leaves. This holds in moisture and minimizes weeds. It also provides a nice place to walk when the rest of the garden is muddy. In fall, all this is organic mulch.

Nita Young NEBO, NC

Whenever you deadhead your plants, throw the flower heads back into the garden. You'll often get free flowers the following spring! I get free snapdragons, petunias, marigolds, alyssum, nicotiana, cosmos, hollyhocks, poppies and more. If you don't like where the new flowers come up, just move them or weed them out.

Peg Lair KENYON, MN

To protect perennials from harsh winters, cover beds with landscape cloth. This allows moisture and air through while still protecting the plants. Since it blocks light, remove it as soon as plants start growing in spring. Cleanup is easy. Even my tea roses do well under this covering.

Roberta Card-Clark
SUPERIOR, WI

Radishes

Each fall, I put several loads of manure and all our leaves and clippings into the garden. It doesn't seem to matter whether the manure is fresh or composted. We get the same good results either way.

David Halbrook KINGS BEACH, CA

I spread and till compost and manure on my garden, then cover the surface with newspapers and straw. In spring, there are no weeds to pull, and the garden is immediately ready to plant.

Dorothy Simons BREMERTON, WA

In areas with mild winters, try this fall routine for a weed-free garden next spring. Pull the spent vegetation from your garden beds, work in compost you've been saving since spring, and mulch with a heavy covering of marsh hay or straw. In spring, just pull back the hay, and you're ready to plant your garden.

Ruth Weaver JOSHUA, TX

The clay in our garden soil tends to become packed. Adding maple leaves in fall helps keep it loose and moist.

Mary Mahn RAVENNA, IL

If you don't want to dig up dahlia tubers each fall, try my method. After the first frost, I cut down the dahlia stalks, place three layers of cardboard over the bed of tubers and cover it with 3 to 4 inches of soil to hold the cardboard in place. Then I top that with 6 to 8 inches of leaves. After all danger of frost has passed in spring, I remove the leaves, soil and cardboard. If the tips of the plants are already peeking through the soil, I cover them with leaves or soil to protect them. With this method, I seldom lose any plants in my Zone 6 area, near Dayton. (Gardeners in more northerly areas should play it safe and bring tubers inside for winter.)

Ethel Gepford MIAMISBURG, OH

LEFT: TERRY WILD/TERRY WILD STOCK; RIGHT: BILL JOHNSON

While you're doing a little bit of yard work this fall, don't just toss all your leaves. Save a few of the nice ones for some fun craft projects. For example, you can do leaf rubbings with kids, string a few together with thread for a fall garland display or make colorful prints with paint (the leaves make great stamps).

Carolyn Hansen JOHNSTON, SC

Before storing them ahead of winter, I dust gladiolus corms and dahlia tuberous roots with sulfur. (For safety, always label treated bulbs.) I store the glad corms in open trays and dahlia roots in boxes of peat moss, and I've seldom had any of them go bad during storage.

Joyce Cooksey BRAINTREE, MA

Once you start cleaning up your garden in fall, you might be surprised at all the clay pots you've acquired. Don't toss them! Clean them up and give them a paint job; they just might make the perfect Christmas gift. (Chalkboard paint is a fun and easy way to give them a new life.)

Kate Folly SAN ANTONIO, TX

I live between two large bodies of water, where we have some wild winter storms and a lot of snow. In the fall, I bag all of my leaves and stack them around the foundation of my house for added insulation. In spring, the leaves are the perfect mulch for my organic vegetable and flower garden.

Lauri Walker SAUBLE BEACH, ON

Eastern wahoo in fall

CHAPTER 4

Winter

Make your green thumb thrive during the cold season with garden do's and don'ts—and watch your frosty backyard come alive with some much-needed color against the gray sky.

All About Hollies

These native plants dazzle with bright berries and glossy green leaves while attracting wildlife to gardens throughout the seasons

By Rachael Liska

Tufted titmouse on winterberry holly

Avoid using English holly as outdoor decor, as birds can eat and spread the seeds.

IT'S HIGH TIME YOU MAKE THE HOLLY FAMILY'S ACQUAINTANCE. Whether you're looking for a cultivar to stun year-round, a berry-producing powerhouse to beckon birds, or a natural hedge to create some privacy between you and your neighbors, hollies feel at home in any landscape.

Festive Past

From ancient winter solstice celebrations to modern-day holiday decor, holly has been a part of our festivities for thousands of years.

With its glossy green leaves that promise evergreen beauty and its bright red berries—technically drupes—English holly (*Ilex aquifolium*) is the plant best known for decking our halls and brightening up winter's dark days. It is native to Europe, Asia and northern Africa and invasive in some parts of the United States. But, with so many wonderful native hollies, you have no need to plant English holly.

Berry Fanatics

Look for these birds that love to feast on holly fruits throughout fall and winter.

- American robins
- Blue jays
- Cedar waxwings
- Eastern bluebirds
- Gray catbirds
- Hermit thrushes
- Northern cardinals
- Northern mockingbirds

Heaps of Hollies

Holly varieties grow across the globe. With more than 400 species belonging to the genus *Ilex*, hollies thrive in tropical, subtropical and temperate zones. They share a few traits.

"All hollies attract beneficial insects and pollinators in the spring when they bloom," says Sue Hunter, who serves as president of the Holly Society of America. "The flowers on both male and female hollies have a strong, pleasant fragrance."

Keep Hollies Happy

Sue says most evergreen species of hollies are drought resistant, though American holly (*I. opaca*) in particular is tough. "Once established, hollies require little care," she says. "Fertilizer can be applied in the spring or fall once plants are dormant, and pruning is done in winter."

Fruit-producing hollies are usually female

PREVIOUS SPREAD: BILL LEAMAN; THIS SPREAD, LEFT: SERGIO COTOS ARES/ALAMY STOCK PHOTO

American robin on American holly

plants that must be pollinated by a nearby male to produce berries. Be sure to include one or more males for every five females, depending on the type. If you need a male plant to pollinate a female, consider Jim Dandy for early-blooming plants and Southern Gentleman for late bloomers.

It's also worth noting that holly berries, leaves and bark are mildly toxic—something to keep in mind if you have curious pets or young children at home.

All-American Beauty

American holly is a native evergreen tree that naturally grows in deciduous forests in the central and southeastern U.S. It reaches 40 to 60 feet tall and grows in a conical shape that's pleasing in larger landscapes from Zones 5 (with protection) to 9. American holly is also known for being resistant to wind, salt spray and deer.

Recommended American holly cultivars include Dan Fenton, with its large leaves and bright red fruit; Goldie, which offers eye-popping yellow fruit; the heavy-fruiting Miss Helen; and Jersey Princess with its dark, glossy leaves.

Special Perks

Beyond being a host plant for Henry's elfin caterpillars, American holly also attracts bees and butterflies that swarm its greenish white flowers. Birds flock to the female plant's bright red or orange fruits that persist through winter.

Even its gray-white bark, spotted with striking red or tan lichens, garners attention. And the American holly's matte leaves distinguish it from its English cousin.

American holly is rather low maintenance, growing in either part shade or full sun. While it prefers acidic, moist yet well-draining soil, it tolerates a range of growing conditions.

TOP: BONNIE TAYLOR BARRY/SHUTTERSTOCK

Yaupon holly

TOP NATIVE HOLLY PICKS

Though options at nurseries and garden centers vary widely from region to region, keep a lookout for these tried-and-true hollies to add some winter cheer to your yard.

Dahoon holly

ILEX CASSINE, ZONES 7 TO 11

Naturally found in swampy areas, these trees are suited for wetter locations. Foster's Holly No. 2, a dahoon-American holly hybrid, does not require a male pollinator to produce fruit.

Winterberry holly

I. VERTICILLATA, ZONES 3 TO 9

This shrub loses its leaves in winter to reveal a showy display of scarlet berries on bare stems, making it perfect for bird-friendly gardens. Winter Red and Maryland Beauty are prolific fruit producers.

Yaupon holly

I. VOMITORIA, ZONES 7 TO 9

Yaupon's small evergreen leaves can be sheared into a privacy screen or even shaped into a topiary. It grows quickly and generally reaches heights of 10 to 20 feet, but in some cases can tower to 30 feet.

Inkberry holly

I. GLABRA, ZONES 4 TO 9

A rounded shrub boasting small black berries that appeal to songbirds and small mammals. Watch for some leaf browning in colder areas.

Possumhaw holly

I. DECIDUA, ZONES 5 TO 9

This deciduous holly grows anywhere from 7 to 15 feet high. Sue suggests pruning Warren's Red into a small tree and underplanting it with perennials such as Virginia bluebells and aromatic aster.

Dahoon holly

Inkberry holly

Possumhaw holly

Blue jays on winterberry holly

INKBERRY: COURTESY OF PROVEN WINNERS - WWW.PROVENWINNERS.COM

Jolly & Festive Planters

Top tips to design a whimsical winter container with materials from your yard

By Rachel Maidl

Choose a container that can handle cold winter temperatures.

WHETHER YOU PREFER SIMPLE or dazzling, you can create a Martha Stewart–worthy planter for your holiday porch with items from the garden and garage.

Katherine Kinch, founder and designer of Your Space by Design in Calgary, Alberta, offers some suggestions to take your arrangements to the next level.

Stay in Sight

Front-door planters greet visitors, but other placements are also worthwhile. Katherine says, "Consider exterior areas such as decks or patios that have clear sightlines from interior spaces." That way you can enjoy them inside, too, no matter how low temperatures go.

Get in Groups

One container is a focal point, but multiple pots are a party. Be creative in how you arrange your planters and displays.

"You will see matching planters on each side of the door," she says. "But a less predictable but fun option is to layer planters of different sizes."

Pick the Right Pot

Katherine points out that not all containers can handle cold winter temperatures. Look for a cast concrete, aluminum, fiberglass or heavy plastic planter to hold your beautiful design.

Add Extras

Simple containers with branches, seed heads and pine cones from the yard provide tons of visual impact. Katherine adds metals or a pop of color with ornaments, berry branches or string lights to make them more festive.

Layer planters of different sizes to add depth and dimension.

Add a small string of white lights to bring a twinkle and glow to winter nights.

TERRYFIC3D, NATTAKORN MANEERAT/EYEEM, IVAYLO IVANOV/EYEEM/GETTY IMAGES (5)

Winter Container Elements

Cedar branches

Lotus seedpods

Juniper branches

Pine cones

Pomegranates

1

PHOTO CREDIT HERE

Creating Winter Interest

Eight bold plants sure to provide a wonderland of color, form and beauty

By Rachael Liska

2

1: DOUGLAS_FREER, 2: BRYTTA/GETTY IMAGES (2)

1. Cotoneaster

Bursting with bright red berries that last through winter, this deer-resistant shrub thrives in cold, windy areas and withstands damage from salt spray. Use it to edge driveways or line retaining walls. With several species available, the options are endless.

2. Boxwood

The workhorse of the winter garden, boxwood adds color and structure. Its natural form is pretty, or you can prune it into a flat hedge or round orb in spring. It also grows easily in containers. Winter Gem is a reliable beauty to consider.

3. Ornamental Grasses

Create intrigue in an otherwise barren garden with elegant stems and plumes that stand at attention and sway with a whisper of winter wind. Grasses also make a terrific source of shelter and food for songbirds. Plant them in masses for big impact and cut them back in early spring. Feather reed grass is a striking, sterile option.

4. Witch Hazel

It's low maintenance, resilient and ignored by most pests. In addition, it provides a wow factor with spidery flowers in hues of yellow, orange, red, copper and purple that bloom from fall or winter into early spring. Not only does this plant light up the dormant landscape, but it's fragrant too. Grow it as a small tree or a large shrub.

4

Witch hazel brings colorful yellow flower clusters to chilly landscapes.

3: TETRA IMAGES, LLC/ALAMY STOCK PHOTO; 4: RDA-GID

5: STEVE AND DAVE MASLOWSKI

5. Crabapple

Best known for presenting a springtime show, these trees also produce red, orange and yellow fruits that appear in fall and persist into winter. They offer a pop of color against snowy gardens and provide food for birds. For a small yard, consider Tina or Firebird. Both are disease resistant with vibrant fruits.

6. Red Twig Dogwood

With red branches that look like coral in a wintry sea, this cold-hardy native stuns. At home in woodland and rain gardens, it shines in every season. Cut old stems back in spring to optimize color on new growth.

6

Beyond winter, red twig dogwood pops with flowers and berries in warmer months.

6: IATRAX/GETTY IMAGES

7

Bohemian waxwing

7. Mountain Ash

Its red-orange berry clusters cling through winter and provide much-needed color against a gray sky. In fall, enjoy fernlike leaves that turn yellow to red before dropping. This native is tolerant of strong winds and serves as a vital food source for birds, especially hungry cedar and Bohemian waxwings.

8. Harry Lauder's Walking Stick

This odd-shaped shrub is a real conversation starter, with bright yellow catkins that dangle from twisty branches. Plant it where everyone can appreciate its one-of-a-kind silhouette.

7: LEONID IKAN/SHUTTERSTOCK; 8: STEVE AND DAVE MASLOWSKI

New Year, New Lessons

Brush up on common blunders to be sure this is your most successful gardening season yet

By George Weigel, National Garden Bureau Member

Planting tomatoes and other plants too early means they may come in contact with frost.

WHAT'S THE DIFFERENCE BETWEEN A NEW GARDENER and an experienced one? The experienced gardener has killed way more plants, or so the saying goes. That truism speaks to the fact that gardening is a highly trial-and-error venture. Here are some common missteps most gardeners make, and what to do instead.

Planting Too Early

THE MISTAKE: Cold-climate gardeners are eager to get petunias, tomatoes and other summer annuals and veggies in the ground at the first sight of frost-free weather in spring. You might get a jump on the season some years, but many gardeners have watched tender plants die when a frost follows a warmup or two.

THE FIX: Know your typical last killing frost dates in spring, then wait until at least then to plant frost-tender plants. Wait until the all-time latest frost-free time is approaching and check the 10-day forecast to be sure nothing is even close to a freeze before planting. Just because garden and home centers are selling tender plants when you're there doesn't mean it's time to put them in the ground.

Volcano Mulching

THE MISTAKE: Adding too much mulch around a tree. *Volcano mulching* is the term for placing mulch in a funnel-like mound that runs up against tree trunks. Though even professional landscapers do this, it's detrimental, as it causes bark rot and gives cover to rodents (mice, chipmunks and voles) that chew on bark. Mulch of more than 3 inches—even if not right up against the trunk—harms trees by reducing the amount of oxygen reaching the roots.

LEFT: ELIZABETH HOLLAR/GETTY IMAGES; DAFFODILS: YON MARSH NATURAL HISTORY/ALAMY STOCK PHOTO

When the blooms on your daffodils are spent, resist the urge to tie, cut or mess with the foliage until it has at least started to yellow.

THE FIX: Keep mulch a few inches away from tree trunks, and limit the layers to no more than 3 inches, including any current mulch layers already in place.

Messing with Bulb Foliage While It's Still Green

THE MISTAKE: Removing bulb foliage early. The weeks after tulips, daffodils, hyacinths and other spring bulbs finish blooming are very important because that's when foliage takes in sunlight that provides energy to recharge the bulbs for next year's bloom. You'll interfere with that process by cutting off foliage that's still green or by reducing the surface area by braiding or tying the leaves, as many people do to "neaten" the post-bloom look.

THE FIX: Don't cut, braid, tie or otherwise mess with spring bulb foliage until it's at least started to yellow, which is a signal that most of the season's photosynthesis work has been completed. Doing so too early can weaken the bulbs.

Digging Up Plants That Aren't Dead

THE MISTAKE: In areas with subfreezing winters, you might think crape myrtles, hardy hibiscus, butterfly bushes, figs and other late-to-leaf-out plants are dead when just about everything else is already green and growing. Know that some plants, especially those native to warmer climates, wait until the weather is consistently warm before springing back to life in late spring. Until then, these might look leafless and dead when they're actually just still dormant.

THE FIX: If you're not sure what's normal for your plants, at least wait until the end of May or even mid-June before digging them out. A test: Scratch a little bark off leafless woody plant stems. If there's green underneath, it's likely your plant is still snoozing and is not dead.

Burning the Lawn with Fertilizer

THE MISTAKE: Some chemical fertilizers are strong enough that if they're applied in excess, the nitrogen in them can brown grass. Uneven applications can also cause streakiness. Another familiar miscue is when DIYers dump granular fertilizer into their spreader and spill some on the surrounding lawn, which causes the unsightly lawn patches.

THE FIX: Apply your fertilizer according to the listed amounts on the package. Or switch to organic fertilizers or those that are naturally high in slow-release nitrogen—both of which are far less likely to burn a lawn. Fill the spreaders on the driveway or other hard surface so you can sweep up spills, keeping fertilizer out of storm sewers and waterways.

Wrong: Volcano mulch

Right: This crape myrtle is dormant, not dead.

Wrong: A lawn with fertilizer burn

MULCH, CRAPE MYRTLE: JOE_POTATO; LAWN: STEVEN WHITE/GETTY IMAGES (3)

Cold-Weather Warriors

These tough blooms, shrubs and grasses shine brightest in winter, when they add interest, texture and structure to your space

By Luke Miller

Early Bloomer
Hellebores first blossom around the holidays in warm regions, depending on the species. Expect plants to bloom in early spring in colder climates.

‹ Hellebore

HELLEBORUS, ZONES 4 TO 9

Cold-weather gardens welcome hellebore's cup-shaped blossoms. With its numerous colors, and heights ranging from 1 to 2 feet, this bloomer is sure to enhance most any landscape. Hellebore is a perennial that loves moisture and shade, and you'll probably wish it bloomed all year-round.

Why we love it: This distinctive plant variety is easy to grow and one of the first flowers to emerge in late winter or early spring.

^ Rugosa rose

ROSA RUGOSA, ZONES 2 TO 7

Large, low-maintenance shrubs grow to 6 feet high and wide. The plant's secret winter weapon is its large, tomato-shaped red hips, which show up after it blooms. Wait to prune until early spring and avoid planting in wet soil. It is considered invasive in some areas, so research before planting.

Why we love it: Dazzling flowers show in early summer, fabulous color in autumn and bright hips in winter.

^ Winter heath

ERICA CARNEA, ZONES 5 TO 7

This evergreen low-growing plant will treat you to an abundance of little purple-pink flowers throughout most of winter and into early spring. Winter heath grows in 6- to 9-inch mounds and creates a dense ground cover over time. It prefers acidic, perfectly drained soil, but it's more tolerant than other heaths.

Why we love it: Glimpsing its small, urn-shaped flowers poking through the snow is delightful.

‹ Snowdrop

GALANTHUS, ZONES 3 TO 8

Always popping up in late winter, snowdrop's bright green leaves send the message loud and clear that spring is right around the corner. For a large collection of these 4- to 6-inch plants, simply lift and divide bulbs after they bloom but before the foliage dies back.

Why we love it: Snowdrops are low maintenance, and they're especially attractive scattered throughout natural gardens and under deciduous trees and shrubs.

WINTER HEATH: RDA-GID; SNOWDROP: AZURE/SHUTTERSTOCK

^ Crocus

VARIETIES INCLUDE *CROCUS ANCYRENSIS* AND *C. TOMMASINIANUS*, ZONES 3 TO 8

In late winter, keep your eyes peeled for these purple, yellow and white flowers poking out of a bed of mulch or beneath a snowy blanket. Plant large drifts of corms in fall for stunning color the next season.

Why we love it:
Known for their strong scent, crocuses help support and attract the first bees and other pollinators emerging from hibernation.

^ Dwarf iris

VARIETIES INCLUDE *IRIS DANFORDIAE* AND *I. RETICULATA*, ZONES 3 TO 9

Reaching just 3 to 9 inches in height, this group of diminutive irises brings bursts of jewel-toned color to late winter and early spring landscapes. Native to Turkey and Iran, they prefer well-draining soil and do best in full sun or partial shade. For an even earlier show, force the bulbs indoors in October or November.

Why we love it: The blooms offer beautiful early color accompanied by a wonderful fragrance.

› Early scilla

SCILLA MISCHTSCHENKOANA, ZONES 4 TO 7

If you're into cool hues, seek out early scilla. This compact green plant sports star-shaped white blossoms striped with blue. They grow in full sun to light shade and spread by offsets and self-seeding. Plant early scilla bulbs in autumn for a spectacular sight come late winter to early spring.

Why we love it: It's a snap to maintain and often continues to flower annually.

› Ornamental cabbage

BRASSICA OLERACEA, ANNUAL

This unusual ornamental flaunts vibrant shades of purple, green, blue, red, pink or white well into winter. Grow in full sun to partial shade. In Zone 7 and warmer, the cabbage is a biennial plant. Try its colorful cousin, ornamental kale, for similar results.

Why we love it: The lower that temps plunge, the more vivid this unique vegetable's colors become.

CROCUS: MARALEE PARK; DWARF IRIS : RDA-GID; EARLY SCILLA: NICK PECKER/SHUTTERSTOCK;

^ Scotch heather

CALLUNA VULGARIS, ZONES 5 TO 7

Celebrated throughout Europe, heather is often forgotten in North America. This versatile flower boasts color in every season; just grow it in acidic soil. Where snowfall is light, insulate heather with mulch and pine branches. **Why we love it:** This beauty lends appeal with florets in summer and autumn, and gorgeous foliage in winter.

SCOTCH HEATHER: BESJUNIOR/SHUTTERSTOCK; PRAIRIE DROPSEED: WALTERS GARDENS, INC

› Prairie dropseed

SPOROBOLUS HETEROLEPIS, ZONES 3 TO 9

This grass's fine-textured, hairlike leaves cluster in green mounds 2 to 3 feet tall and wide. When its seeds mature in autumn, they drop to the ground from their hulls, giving the plant its common name. The grass provides beautiful structure in winter and grows in a range of soils. For best results, plant in sandy or loamy plots in full sun. It is drought tolerant and native to many areas in the U.S.
Why we love it: Thin strands fade to light bronze in the winter, creating a wonderful border or foundation plant.

Spread Cheer

Holiday decor doesn't have to stay indoors. Boost the winter appeal of blue spruce and other large evergreen trees with festive lights, ornaments or garland.

‹ Blue spruce

PICEA PUNGENS, ZONES 2 TO 7

Blue spruce is a large tree, but small shrublike cultivars max out at 5 to 15 feet high. The blue-gray foliage is particularly alluring in the winter landscape, when a dash of color is sorely needed. For a more blue color, select one of several cultivars known for their intense blue color.

Why we love it: The lovely foliage, but also the range of shapes—mounded to lollipop to pompom.

^ Winterberry

ILEX VERTICILLATA, ZONES 3 TO 9

Grown as a small tree or a shrub, winterberry doesn't get much attention during the growing season. Come winter, though, this wallflower demands to be seen when it bursts to life with bright red berries.

Why we love it: The impressive collection of fruit lasts for months—if the songbirds don't gobble it up first. Plant winterberry in groups for big impact.

^ Paperbark maple

ACER GRISEUM, ZONES 4 TO 8

Like many other maples, paperbark has showy, orange to red fall foliage. To ease your pain when the show is over, the tree delivers shiny, coppery peeling bark in winter. Many gardeners intentionally "limb them up," which means to remove lower branches so there's more of the bright bark in view.

Why we love it: It's a good-looking tree that tolerates partial shade. Grow this maple where it can be enjoyed!

‹ Redtwig and yellowtwig dogwood

CORNUS SERICEA, ZONES 2 TO 7

Dogwoods display flowers in spring and respectable leaf color in fall. However, redtwig and yellowtwig dogwood are really known for their bark. Remove older stems every few years, because the youngest growth produces the most color.

Why we love it: Dogwoods are easy to maintain, requiring little more than annual pruning.

PAPERBARK MAPLE: CHRIS CLARK/ALAMY STOCK PHOTO

^ Pink muhly grass

MUHLENBERGIA CAPILLARIS, ZONES 5 TO 9

Many ornamental grasses provide exceptional winter interest, but muhly grass, also known as pink hair grass, gets a nod for its distinctive airy and pink flowers that bloom into late fall. After that, the drama continues as the plant sways in the winter wind.

Why we love it: Muhly grass is simple to grow, tolerates poor soil, looks great in masses and survives drought conditions.

^ Witch hazel

HAMAMELIS SPP., ZONES 3 TO 9

Is it overstating things to say witch hazel is, ahem, bewitching? Not when you see it unfurl its spider-like flowers in middle to late winter. All but autumn witch hazel (a fall bloomer) are bare when in bloom, making the golden yellow, sometimes reddish orange flowers more conspicuous.

Why we love it: Witch hazels are tough, undemanding shrubs with stunning fall foliage and winter flowers.

› Coral bark Japanese maple

ACER PALMATUM 'SANGO KAKU,' ZONES 5 TO 8

The coral-orange-red bark is brightest and most noticeable in winter. Ample moisture, afternoon shade and protection from winds help keep coral bark maple looking its best.

Why we love it: The bark's unique color. And this slow-growing, relatively small tree is a perfect fit in almost any garden.

› Hinoki false cypress

CHAMAECYPARIS OBTUSA, ZONES 4 TO 8

This little gem isn't so little in its native Japan, where it reaches 70 feet tall. Most nursery-grown cultivars are shorter than 10 feet, making them a perfect fit for small backyard gardens.

Why we love it: The tightly packed, swirly, golden green foliage makes hinoki false cypress an absolute rock star, especially in winter.

MUHLY GRASS: PAUL BRENNAN/SHUTTERSTOCK; WITCH HAZEL: LIANEM/SHUTTERSTOCK;

^ Harry Lauder's walking stick

CORYLUS AVELLANA 'CONTORTA,' ZONES 3 TO 9

This small, contorted shrublike tree is known to make people long for winter. Sure, there's golden yellow foliage in fall, but once the leaves drop, the artistry of its gnarled shape steals the show.
Why we love it: The twisty gray branches are an architectural sensation and look particularly beautiful when covered in a dusting of snow.

› Flowering crabapple

MALUS SPP., ZONES 4 TO 8

This beloved backyard tree offers year-round interest. Outstanding spring blooms and brightly colored red, orange or yellow fruit in fall and winter are crabapple's top selling points.
Why we love it: It comes in a range of forms. The newer cultivars are disease resistant and yield more colorful fruit.

WALKING STICK: MÜLLER/MCPHOTO/ALAMY STOCK PHOTO; CRABAPPLE: NALIDSA/SHUTTERSTOCK

How Do You Keep Gardening in Winter?

Readers share clever ways they keep their thumbs green this time of year

Geranium

I plant a cover crop of cereal rye alongside broccoli and Brussels sprouts.

Mike Buckler RINGGOLD, GA

Since I live in Florida, gardening for me is a year-round activity. My main concern is watering.

Karen Lynn PLANT CITY, FL

Lots of flower catalogs help me plan for an even better flower bed the coming year.

Ginny Price TAYLORS, SC

I bring in my pots of geraniums, cut them back and set them on the windowsill in the basement. The plants get watered when I do laundry, and they seem to be quite happy.

Mary Clark GREENSBURG, PA

In winter, we compost our biodegradable matter. Coffee grounds, eggshells, vegetables and fruit all contribute to the pile. We aerate it with a pitch fork.

Sue Steele ESSEX, MD

My houseplants spend the warmer months outdoors, but I bring them in during the cold months. They add a little green to winter. This year, I have some potted herbs I'm keeping indoors.

Megan Long RED WING, MN

TOP: LETTY17, BOTTOM: SILVIA JANSEN/GETTY IMAGES (2)

Geraniums

Violas

Geraniums are my favorites! I have two that I over-winter every year. I use them to propagate plants for next summer.

Rebecca Williamson BUSHNELL, IL

I go online and sign up for all the free seed books. The heirloom ones are the most fun.

Patrick Hogan TEMPERANCE, MI

I have tons of plants in my sunroom, including a 6-foot-tall avocado tree. After buds form in late winter, I bring forsythia branches indoors and put them in water. Sometimes they bloom!

Melanie Theisen RIDGE, NY

I use the cold months to prepare for gardening season. I research heirlooms and new veggies, sharpen tools, and plan new flower bed layouts.

Kathy Eppers ALEDO, TX

I plant cool-weather spinach, violas and snap-dragons in grow boxes on my deck. Not only do I have nutritious food all winter, but I also have beautiful flowers to brighten each day!

Sandra Sykes WESTMINSTER, SC

We use dead and dried flower stalks and seed pods as perches for winter birds at our feeders.

Suzanne Cassidy HUGHESVILLE, MD

TOP: LYNEA, BOTTOM: ELENA KUZNETSOVA/SHUTTERSTOCK (2)

Top Tools

Use hand pruners when removing stems less than ¾ inch thick. Bypass pruners are preferred because they result in a clean cut.

TOP LEFT: GARY BLAKE/ALAMY STOCK PHOTO; THIS IMAGE: KRISTINA POKALUK/GETTY IMAGES

Become a Pruning Pro

Get the job done right with advice from an experienced gardener

By Niki Jabbour

FOR MOST DECIDUOUS TREES AND SHRUBS, winter is the best time for pruning. Plants are dormant and bare, so it's easier to see their branching structure and get a sense of what needs to be removed. It's also better for the plants because winter pruning promotes quick regrowth in spring and limits the exposure of the wounds to insects and disease.

The first rule of pruning is this: Don't prune unless you have a good reason. One reason could be the appearance. You might have a young plant like a fruit tree and want to train it into an open canopy and balanced shape. Or maybe you want to control the size of a shrub to ensure it doesn't outgrow its space. A major reason for pruning is to encourage flowering or increase fruit production, especially in plants like forsythia and highbush blueberry. Finally, branches that are dead, broken or hanging are a safety hazard, so it's best to get them out of the way.

Pruning can be an intimidating task for a lot of gardeners, but pruning mistakes are similar to a bad haircut: It may look funny for a while, but it'll surely grow back. Here are some pro tips to help you tackle winter pruning.

Prune and Shape

In order to keep vining plants like this climbing hydrangea looking great, use pole pruners for hard-to-reach spaces.

DO's

DO pick a dry, sunny day, which is more comfortable for you and beneficial for the plant. Wet plants can spread disease.

DO start with clean, sharp tools. If you remove diseased tissue from a plant, wipe your pruning tools with a 10% bleach solution between cuts.

DO study the shape of the plant and consider each cut before you start pruning.

DO start by always removing the three D's—dead, damaged or diseased wood.

DO take out any crossing branches. Rubbing injures plant tissue and invites disease. Typically, the smaller of the two branches is removed.

DO remove water sprouts and suckers. Suckers grow from the base of the trunk or the roots of trees, while water sprouts emerge from branches. Both are vigorous, fast-growing shoots, but they tend to interfere with healthy growth, flowering and fruiting. Often, water sprouts on fruit trees also block air and sunlight, reducing fruiting and increasing the risk of wounds and disease.

DO trim long, unbranched stems back to a healthy, outward-facing bud. This is called heading and will stimulate nearby side buds and branches to grow.

DO prune overgrown or bushy trees and shrubs by making thinning cuts, the most common type of cut. This will allow more light and air to reach the center of the plant. To thin, prune the branch or stem back to its point of origin at the base of the plant, a main stem or the trunk.

DO take frequent breaks to step back and study the plant to make sure your pruning looks balanced and natural.

Use a lopper tool for stems up to 1¾ inches thick.

CLOCKWISE FROM LEFT: TERRY WILD/TERRY WILD STOCK (2); RUDIGOBBO/GETTY IMAGES

DON'Ts

DON'T leave unsightly stubs, which can become diseased or infested with insects. Instead, prune to a healthy out-facing bud or branch.

DON'T shear shrubs into unnatural shapes unless you wish to create a formal hedge or topiary. Trees and shrubs look best when allowed to grow to their natural shape and size.

DON'T overprune. A rule of thumb is to remove no more than a fourth to a third of the canopy per year.

DON'T be shy about pruning mature neglected shrubs. Multistemmed shrubs like lilacs, forsythias and dogwoods can be rejuvenated with the gradual removal of old wood. Begin by pruning a fourth to a third of the old stems. Repeat each year until all the old wood is removed.

DON'T cut tree limbs flush to the trunk. Instead, cut the branch where it meets the branch collar. This will promote quick and healthy callusing of the wound and there is no need for pruning paint.

DON'T forget safety! Always wear eye protection. Never prune plants close to power lines or try to remove the branches that can't be reached with a pole pruner. Instead, call the experts!

Tough Trees
Flowering dogwoods and other trees need a pruning saw to manage branches that are too large for hand pruners or loppers.

CLASSICSTOCK/ALAMY STOCK PHOTO

What to Prune in Winter

- Summer-flowering shrubs and trees such as rose of Sharon, crape myrtle, potentilla, smoke bush, butterfly bush and beautyberry. They produce flower buds on new growth and respond well to dormant pruning in winter. Shrubs grown for foliage, such as barberry, privet and burning bush, are also good candidates for winter pruning.
- Deciduous fruit trees such as apples, pears, cherries and plums. Dormant pruning removes some of the flower buds, but it also opens up the tree to more light and air, boosting tree health and fruit size and quality.
- Fruiting shrubs such as highbush blueberries, currants and gooseberries. Remove the oldest stems at ground level to encourage fresh fruiting branches.
- Deciduous trees like oak, honey locust and linden. As with smaller shrubs and trees, it's easier to see the framework of the branches in the winter.

What Not to Prune in Winter

- Spring-flowering shrubs and trees like forsythia, lilac, quince, bigleaf hydrangea, rhododendron and azalea, which form their flower buds on wood from the previous year. These are best pruned after flowering in spring.
- Trees with heavy winter sap flow like maples, dogwoods and birches. Sap loss won't hurt the trees, but it can make a sticky mess on nearby structures, cars or furniture. These trees are easier to prune in midsummer when sap flow isn't a problem.
- Most conifers should be pruned during their growth spurt in late spring. Do research on specific conifers for tips.

Words of Wisdom

Dig into these pro tips and tricks perfect for budding gardeners

Always remember that gardening is an experiment with many variables, and the results are never permanent. Try a small-scale project like a large container, an herb garden, a vegetable patch or a few plants along the foundation of your home. Don't be fearful of mistakes; they can always be fixed.

Pat Northington AUSTIN, TX

Start small with a variety of perennials for early spring, summer and fall so that your garden blooms all-year round. Also, get involved in the Master Gardener program. Its members offer great advice and you can sometimes get cuttings of unique plants.

Toni Meyers CHILI, WI

Buy the best gardening tools you can find and take good care of them so they last. I inherited some spades, trowels and hoes from my mother nearly 30 years ago, and I'm still using them.

Leda Klein BYRON, NY

Get a good reference book for your zone. Make sure it has lots of pictures and information. It's worth its weight in gold. Mine is dog-eared, and the pages are dirty and worn, but I wouldn't trade it for all the internet sites in the world.

Arlene Tencza WAXHAW, NC

Look around at businesses to see what landscapers have planted and what the highway department is growing in medians. These low-maintenance plants will give you a good foundation.

Doreen Damm NEW PORT RICHEY, FL

Did You Know?

You can save space in the garden by growing veggies with vertical trellises. Try climbers such as cucumbers and pole beans.

CHAPTER 5

Indoor Gardening

Worried about keeping your indoor plants happy through winter or while you're on vacation? Here are the ultimate low-maintenance houseplant hacks to liven up your living spaces.

Houseplant Rescue

Help is here! The *Birds & Blooms* garden pro offers solutions to the most common indoor plant problems.

By Melinda Myers

THE FIRST STEP IN TREATING YOUR plants is to understand the likely dilemmas and their solutions. Here are a few common questions I receive about ailing houseplants and how to address them. Once you know what to look for, you'll be surprised by how quickly your diagnostic skills improve.

Why Are the Leaves Yellow?

Start by evaluating your regular watering habits. Watering too frequently or infrequently can cause leaves to yellow. Tropical plants prefer moist soil, while cacti and succulents like the soil to go dry between watering. Always use your finger to check the top 1 or 2 inches of soil for moisture before watering.

Increase success by using containers with drainage holes or self-watering pots with weep holes that allow excess water to escape. Pour off any water that collects in the saucer to avoid root rot, or place pebbles in the saucer to elevate the pot above the excess water.

Once you've ruled out improper watering, it's time to review your fertilization schedule. Let the plants be your guide. Pale, yellow or stunted leaves may mean the plants need a nutrient boost. Use a diluted solution of houseplant fertilizer and only fertilize actively growing plants from spring through early fall, even if they're always indoors.

Mites, aphids and scale pests suck plant juices, causing the leaves to yellow and turn brown. A strong blast of water dislodges many of the insects. A couple of applications of insecticidal soap will also manage these pests and immature scale insects. Organic horticulture oil labeled for use on houseplants is effective at controlling pests at all stages.

Golden pothos

Snake plant

What Do Brown Edges Mean?

If your plant is sporting crispy, dark edges, it may mean you need to water more often. Check the soil moisture, and slowly reduce the number of days in between watering. Watch your plants for signs of improvement.

Lack of humidity could also be the cause. Tropical plants prefer higher humidity than we have in our homes. When we turn on the heat in winter, there's even less moisture in the air. Group plants together so that as one loses moisture through its leaves, the neighbors benefit. Or place plants on saucers or trays filled with pebbles and water. Set a pot on the pebbles above the water. As water evaporates, it increases the humidity around the plant, where it is needed.

Why Is My Plant Spindly and Leaning?

Light is likely the cause of these problems. Give plants a quarter turn every few weeks to promote even growth. Let in more light if plants have thin stems and excessive space between each set of leaves.

Plants that need a lot of light thrive when placed in front of an east- or west-facing window. Low-light plants can be 6 feet back, off to the side of these windows or near a north-facing one. Once you provide the right amount of light, pinch off the growing tips of leggy plants to encourage compact growth.

What Are These Spots?

Brown, black and water-soaked spots on leaves and stems often indicate that a fungal or bacterial disease is the problem.

Adjust the watering schedule and do not allow plants to sit in excess water. Often that alone is enough to stop the disease's progress. Remove and dispose of any soft, discolored stems and leaves. Trim off any rotten roots and repot in fresh potting mix in a container slightly larger than the remaining roots.

Chinese evergreen

PREVIOUS SPREAD: SWITLANA SONYASHNA/SHUTTERSTOCK; THIS SPREAD, CLOCKWISE FROM TOP LEFT: GRAPHICDNA, TETIANA GARKUSHA/GETTY IMAGES (2); VISIONS BV, NETHERLANDS/VISIONSPICTURES & PHOTOGRAPHY

Cast iron plant

Philodendron

Why Are the New Leaves Small?

When new leaves are smaller than normal, the plant could be pot-bound or may need to be fertilized or moved to a brighter location. Look for other clues when making your diagnosis.

If the water runs out of the pot quickly and roots are filling the container, it's time to move your plant to the next size container. Avoid moving pot-bound plants to much larger containers, which can potentially slow down above-ground growth and lead to root rot. If the pot size seems adequate, evaluate your fertilizer schedule and light.

What's the Sticky Stuff?

Pests such as mites, aphids, scale and mealy bugs drink up plant juices, secreting the excess. This clear sticky substance is called honeydew and is often the first clue these pests are feeding on your plants. As I described earlier, try rinsing off the bugs first. If that doesn't get rid of them, move on to insecticidal soap or organic horticulture oil labeled for houseplants.

How Do I Get Rid of the Small Flies?

Fungus gnats are not harmful but certainly are annoying. The immature gnats feed on organic matter in the soil, while the adult flies flit around your home.

To evict them, allow the soil to go a bit drier and trap the adults with a container of apple cider vinegar on the countertop. You could also use organic *Bacillus thuringiensis israelensis*, which is in Mosquito Bits. Sprinkle the product over the soil surface and repeat as often as the label directions recommend.

Tough as Nails

Match these plants with the right amount of sun and water to expect success.

- Snake plant (*Sanseveria* spp.)
- Philodendron
- Pothos
- Chinese evergreen
- Cast iron plant
- ZZ plant

ZZ plant

RFISHER27, KSENIIA SOLOVEVA/GETTY IMAGES (2); NEW AFRICA/SHUTTERSTOCK

Watering Made Easy

Keep houseplants satisfied with systems that do the work for you

By Helen Newling Lawson

YANA FEFELOVA/SHUTTERSTOCK

WATERING PLANTS INSIDE a dry home, especially in winter, can turn into a daily chore. Houseplant watering systems are here to save the day and keep you and your plants happy by providing consistent and controlled moisture, without overwatering. To pick the right solution, all you need to know is how much water your plants need.

Try these handy gadgets—they'll keep watering to a minimum while keeping your plants looking their best.

Spikes and Globes

These simple devices let water slowly drip into the soil. Watering spikes require a glass or plastic bottle to act as a reservoir. Watering globes are an all-in-one solution, and many have a pretty blown-glass look. Depending on the size of your container, you may need several spikes or globes to keep your plant evenly watered. These are best for plants that like to stay continually moist.

Self-Watering Containers

These handy pots feature a built-in reservoir in the base of the planter that allows water to be pulled into the soil as it dries. One downside is that they typically need refilling every few days. Most models recommended for houseplants are made of solid-colored plastic, but those designed for outdoor use may give you more options.

Humidity Mats

Water-soaked mats placed in trays below the plants or on top of the soil keep moisture levels steady. Tray mats work best with terra-cotta pots but may dry out quickly in direct sunlight. Rings that rest on the soil are visible and might be unsightly, so add some mulch to disguise them.

Soil Additives

Pellets added to the potting mix absorb and then slowly release water back into the soil to reduce the need to water. Some are made from water-storing polymers, or you can try ones made of biodegradable wool. Do not use these in combination with systems that wick water into the soil; the water-retaining ability of these additives will pull more moisture than your plants probably need.

Smart Ways to Keep Plants Happy

Top picks to make watering a breeze

Indoor Hose
This mini coil hose (also shown above) with sprayer attaches to a kitchen sink faucet.
gardeners.com

HydroSpike
Similar to watering spikes, these have a flexible tube that pulls from a larger container for less frequent refills.
hydrospike.com

Wool Pellets
These reduce watering needs by 25% and also deliver a gentle feeding from natural nutrients in the wool.
wildvalleyfarms.com

Drip Irrigation Systems

As a more complex setup, a drip irrigation system supplies a slow flow of water via an emitter attached to tubes. Plants must be close enough to the device for the tubes to reach. Built-in timers can be adjusted for plants that enjoy a dry spell.

FROM TOP: PHOTO COURTESY OF GARDENER'S SUPPLY COMPANY (2); HYDROSPIKE; WILD VALLEY FARMS

Easy-Care Succulents

Fun and funky houseplants add flair to an indoor space

By Hannah Pugh

STRING OF BANANAS: BARBARA RICH/GETTY IMAGES; PANDA PLANT: LITTLE PRINCE OF OREGON NURSERY WWW.LITTLEPRINCEPLANTS.COM;

‹ String of bananas

CURIO RADICANS

Perfect for an indoor hanging planter, this succulent's tendrils are covered with small leaves that are shaped like little green bananas. Place it in a spot that receives plenty of sunlight, with a lot of room for it to cascade down, such as the top of a bookshelf.

Why we love it: Give the plant some time outside during warmer months, if desired, by gradually acclimating it.

^ Panda plant

KALANCHOE TOMENTOSA

It's very easy to care for this succulent, which is also known as chocolate soldier. Let the soil completely dry out between waterings. Because panda plant stores plenty of water in its thick, fuzz-covered leaves, that means less watering for you.

Why we love it: The soft, velvety texture over light green leaves with dark tips pops when the plant gets enough light.

^ Ponytail palm

BEAUCARNEA RECURVATA

The ponytail palm succulent has a thick, trunklike stem that sprouts stringy green leaves from the top. It prefers a sunny spot and needs very little watering, about once every three to four weeks. It's also nontoxic for both cats and dogs, so you can quite safely place one on your floor.

Why we love it: Though the name suggests otherwise, this plant is not a tree—it just looks like one!

‹ Crown of thorns

EUPHORBIA MILII

Tiny, usually pink or red flowers bloom almost year-round on this plant, adding a splash of color to any blank space in your home. Wear tough gloves when planting crown of thorns in a pot of well-draining soil, as its thorns are sharp. Give it a spot near a window so it gets several hours of direct sunlight.

Why we love it: A wide variety of hybrid cultivars are available, including Mini-Bell for small pots or Rosalie and Saturnus for extra-large flowers.

^ African milk tree

EUPHORBIA TRIGONA

A tall and easy-to-care-for succulent, the African milk tree has small teardrop-shaped leaves, as well as thorns that grow vertically along the ridges of thick green stems. Because of its sharp thorns and irritating sap, it's not recommended for homes with children or pets.

Why we love it: This plant adds some height and drama to your space. It reaches 5 or 6 feet indoors, although it can be pruned shorter.

^ Prickly pear cactus

OPUNTIA SPP.

One fun fact about prickly pear cactus: It's a cinch to propagate. Though some prickly pears are hardy enough for outdoor gardens, any that are kept inside thrive best where they can get bright light and stay warm.

Why we love it: Like most other cactuses, the prickly pear generally requires little maintenance.

› Hens-and-chicks

SEMPERVIVUM SPP.

A classic in the world of succulents, hens-and-chicks starts out very small and is easy to propagate. With rosettes in a variety of greens and reds, the plants look amazing grouped with other types of succulents in a pot.

Why we love it: Try planting hens-and-chicks outside in the garden too—it is hardy in Zones 4 to 8.

AFRICAN MILK TREE: MILART/SHUTTERSTOCK; PRICKLY PEAR CACTUS: EKSPANSIO/GETTY IMAGES; HENS-AND-CHICKS: TAEWAFEEL/SHUTTERSTOCK

^ Zebra plant

HAWORTHIOPSIS FASCIATA

The zebra plant is an eye-catching dark green succulent with white horizontal stripes along its spiky leaves. The small plant grows slowly and can withstand long periods without water. Let the soil completely dry between waterings; it won't tolerate overwatering. Place the plant near an east-facing window for best results.

Why we love it: Zebra plant is quite easy to keep alive indoors because it can handle very dry air.

^ Aloe

ALOE VERA

Similar to other succulents, aloe does just fine with indirect sunlight in a home. And it isn't fazed by dry indoor air. Keep it in sandy, well-draining soil. Mature aloe plants may produce flowers.

Why we love it: Break off a piece of aloe vera and use the clear liquid inside to soothe a burn or irritated skin.

STRING OF PEARLS: INSUNG JEON/GETTY IMAGES

‹ String of pearls

CURIO ROWLEYANUS

This funky, medium-sized succulent grows skinny stems of vibrant green, pearl-like leaves. It prefers a lot of sun and, like many other succulents, is very easy to propagate. Make sure it has soil that drains well, and don't overwater. Wear gloves when handling to avoid skin irritation.

Why we love it: Place string of pearls on a high shelf in your home so it drapes over the side of its container. Its tendrils can stretch 2 to 3 feet long.

Nurturing Holiday Cheer

How to keep your Christmas cactus happy and healthy

By Mikayla Borchert

Adjust light and temperature to encourage more blooms.

FROM LEFT: KARENHBLACK, PETROVVAL/GETTY IMAGES (2)

A CHRISTMAS CACTUS IS both a colorful houseplant and a great holiday gift for novice and expert gardeners alike. It is low maintenance and pet friendly, with brilliant, usually pink blooms that delight.

To help a Christmas cactus thrive and flower, there are several best practices to keep in mind. With some TLC, these beauties flourish indoors, growing to incredible sizes.

North- and east-facing windows provide ideal light.

Pick a Pot

Start by checking the size of your container. If the pot is too large, you'll have fewer flowers, so don't size up by more than a couple of inches. Don't repot while the plant is blooming either, or you'll lose all the flowers in the process. This plant likes crowded roots, so you won't need to swap containers very often.

Right Light

A perk for people with dim indoor spaces: The succulents do best in indirect light. Place plants near a north- or east-facing window. A Christmas cactus can tolerate some direct sunlight, but be mindful of the hot afternoon sun. Too much light will discolor the leaves.

If you notice burning, gently move the plant away from the window. The flowers are delicate and fall off easily, so try to avoid rearranging when the cactus is in bloom.

Water Well

Plant the Christmas cactus in well-draining soil, then water only when the top 1 or 2 inches are dry. Use a succulent- or houseplant-specific plant food between blooms to fuel fresh bud growth.

Humidity will also help your cactus thrive, especially in the winter. Place it near other plants or put rocks in the tray and add a shallow layer of water, so it doesn't touch the container, to increase moisture in the air.

Bring on the Blooms

Colorful flowers make the Christmas cactus a showstopper. And, with a little planning, you can time the blooms for a special occasion or get the plant to bloom more than once.

The cactus's bloom cycle depends on cues from temperature, light and moisture, so first decide when you'd like your plant to flower. Start about two months before your chosen date. For eight to 10 weeks, give your plant 13 to 15 hours of darkness in a cool environment at night, bringing it back to indirect light during the day. Do not expose it to any artificial light during the dark period. Leaving the soil slightly drier also promotes more blooms.

When you see buds, slowly transition your Christmas cactus to the spot you'd like to display it. The buds will blossom, and you'll be treated to tropical pink flowers.

Cactus or Not?

It's not just a name—the Christmas cactus is a real cactus, although it's different from the ones you'd find in a desert. It's a succulent plant native to Brazil, so it likes more water and humidity than the average cactus. If you tend to overwater other types of cactuses, a Christmas cactus might be a better option for your home.

Indoor Plant Care

From vacation-watering hacks to winter survival tips, readers dish out their best secrets for houseplant TLC

African violet

FROM LEFT: TERRY WILD/TERRY WILD STOCK (2)

Even though it might be cold outside, you can still continue gardening indoors during the winter months. In fact, it's a great time to start your garden early.

In late December and early January, I turn half of my kitchen and dining area into a hothouse, complete with shelving and lights.

I start by planting seeds in egg cartons. Then I cover them with plastic and put them on my shelves. As the plants get taller, I put old toilet paper rolls around the growing plants for some extra support.

After the last frost date passes in spring, I plant my veggies outside. Then I get to enjoy fresh vegetables a lot earlier.

Winter can be a great time to garden—you just have to get a little creative. It's fun to do and will keep you gardening year-round.

Howard Bohne
NORTH CHARLESTON, SC

The refrigerator is an easy spot to store seeds over winter. Simply place thoroughly dried seeds collected from your flower and vegetable gardens in envelopes in plastic bags. Label, seal and into the refrigerator they go! Come spring, you'll be all set for planting.

Elsie Kolberg ST. JOSEPH, MI

When I plant my amaryllis in the garden come summer, I leave them in pots. In fall, I just pull the pots out and bring them in the basement, where they lie on their sides for six to eight weeks. Once the bulbs begin to sprout, I plant them in fresh soil, bring them upstairs and place them in a bright window. Then I give them a good drink to help start their growing season.

Vivian Mccorkle
SMITHVILLE, MO

Our houseplants survived our month-long vacation, even though we didn't have anyone to water them.

I watered the plants thoroughly, then put each one inside its own clear plastic trash bag. I left plenty of air in the bags and tied ribbons around the tops to secure them. I set the plants out of the sun, turned the thermostat down to 55 degrees and took off.

When we returned four weeks later, the flowering plants were blooming. We had 15 plants, and all of them looked beautiful except for one vine that didn't do well.

Mae Biemeret WATERSMEET, MI

My grandmother taught me to save money on annuals by taking "slips" of plants in the fall.

I make cuttings from healthy plants, root them in water or a well-drained potting mix, then grow them in a sunny window all winter. By spring, they're ready to set out.

Sharon Bradshaw
RICHMOND, MO

Mums

FROM LEFT: TERRY WILD/TERRY WILD STOCK (2)

Potted summer flowers in old steel frying pan base

When plant leaves get dusty, clean them with a rag dipped in milk. It leaves them shiny and is much cheaper than commercial sprays.

Diane Lee
RICHLAND CENTER, WI

Use room-temperature or warm water when watering houseplants. This prevents them from going into shock and keeps them healthy.

Darlene Wyness
WILLIAMS LAKE, BC

When changing the water in your aquarium, don't throw it out!

Use it on your houseplants or outdoor plants. It gives them a boost and is much cheaper than commercial fertilizer.

Emma Fraser LUDLOW, ME

Use coffee grounds and leftover coffee on your houseplants and watch them thrive. I've been doing this for a long time, and it really works.

Delores Koland PELICAN RAPIDS, MN

Tulips are easy to force indoors during winter.

Trumpet vine

In fall, pot up leftover spring-flowering bulbs, water and store them in a picnic cooler in an unheated garage. Then, after 12 weeks of cold treatment, bring them indoors and place in a sunny location. They'll start growing and flower in about four weeks.

Howard Baszynski
WAUWATOSA, WI

Wintering geraniums is fairly easy with my method. Before frost hits, pull them up and place them in brown grocery bags. Store under the basement stairs with the bags open. At potting time, trim to 4 to 6 inches, place in pots and put back under the stairs. When plants begin to grow, they're ready to be set outside, but they may need to be protected from the cold.

Josephine Slemmons
JACKSON, MI

I couldn't throw away the poinsettia that my son gave me, so I came up with a way to keep it thriving and blooming. It's easy to do, so if you have a leftover poinsettia, consider giving this a try. It's a great challenge.

After the holidays, I keep my poinsettia in a corner of the house near a sunny window. In spring, I plant it in my rock garden when the temperature remains around 50 degrees. I place the plant, pot and all, in a semi-shaded area. Then I bring it back in the house on the first day of autumn.

Once it's back inside, I use a procedure I call "long night, short day" to get it to bloom again. I keep the poinsettia in complete darkness for 14 continuous hours each night. (Either move it to a dark room or closet, or put a box over it.) Continue this treatment until the bracts are fully colored. With these tips, your plant will be beautiful next year for Christmas!

Loretta Coverdell AMANDA, OH

TULIPS: CAROL L. EDWARDS; TRUMPET VINE: BILL JOHNSON; DRYING FLOWERS: TERRY WILD/TERRY WILD STOCK

Here's how I keep small houseplants moist while on vacation. For each plant, I punch a few small holes in a plastic bag. I enclose each plant in a bag and fasten with a twist-tie after watering. The plants stay moist for up to a few weeks.

Lucille Ruth
PORT CHARLOTTE, FL

Every time I water my houseplants, including my prized bonsai, I rotate the pot a quarter turn. This way new growth comes up evenly, and the plants do not lean in search of light.

Judy Larson GREENDALE, WISCONSIN

Try watering hanging plants with ice cubes. As the ice melts, the soil absorbs the water, and it doesn't drip out of the bottom of the pot.

Roslyn Francis LODI, CA

Hang your herbs for drying in winter. Then blend to make your own herb and spice mixes.

Houseplant Care

Quick facts and tips to ensure you're the best indoor plant parent

3 If you're tight on space, most 3-inch pots fit on even the narrowest windowsills. Peperomia and small cactuses can both happily grow in containers that size.

12 When using artificial lights, the tips of the plants should be 6 to 12 inches from the light source to ensure the plant is receiving maximum benefits.

1/4 To help maintain a symmetrical shape, give houseplants a quarter turn occasionally, maybe even every time you water if it helps you to remember.

50 Ideal humidity for tropical houseplants is around 50%. If your home is drier, set your plants on a gravel tray filled with water.

2 When transplanting a houseplant to a larger pot, an increase of 2 inches in container size is ideal, unless your plant is very large.

10-10-10

Most houseplants do fine with a balanced fertilizer (10-10-10). Limit or stop fertilizing your houseplants in winter and start feeding them again in spring. As always, follow directions on your specific package.

By Eva Monheim

RAWPIXEL.COM/SHUTTERSTOCK

***Tillandsias* are easy-care houseplants.**

500 **There are more than 500 species of *Tillandsia*, which are also called air plants. The nickname comes from their ability to grow in any nook or cranny instead of in soil.**

2 To ensure your plants get the two types of light that they need—red and blue wavelengths—gardeners can use both warm- and cool-toned fluorescent bulbs or an LED plant light.

86 Most indoor plants grow best between 70 and 80 degrees during the day—although some like it hot, tolerating temps up to 86 degrees.

3 Philodendron, aloe and snake plants are three very low-maintenance options for beginners that thrive in different amounts of light.

½ When repotting a houseplant, make sure the soil reaches about a half inch below the pot's edge.

7 African violets, a longtime favorite, come in shades of seven different colors: white, pink, maroon, blue, lavender, violet and deep purple.

18 The wax plant, *Hoya carnosa*, is named after Thomas Hoy, a botanist and gardener for an English duke in the 18th century.

By Emily Hannemann

VISIONS BV, NETHERLANDS

Low-Light Lovers

Easy-to-grow houseplants detoxify and color even the darkest corners of your home

By Dianne Bright

Get Creative
Use air plants in a terrarium to liven up a desk space, or weave them into a festive wreath with branches and berries.

‹ Air plant

TILLANDSIA SPP.

Air plants absorb moisture from the air through their leaves, which is why they typically grow best in humid environments. To promote the health of this low-light houseplant, submerge it in water for 30 minutes every week or two. In nature, air plants cling to branches, bark or bare rocks.

Why we love it: Air plants add a dash of decorative flair to any space. They are commonly seen mounted, placed in a terrarium or set inside charming seashells.

^ English ivy

HEDERA HELIX

Most commonly known as an indoor hanging plant, English ivy can be trained to climb a trellis or moss stick. Stay consistent with watering; ivy prefers evenly moist soil. Mist the leaves to keep them from gathering dust and to prevent spider mites. Improve drainage by placing a gravel-filled saucer under the pot.

Why we love it: There's an ivy for every room. About 30 varieties are available, from plain green to variegated with yellow or gold.

^ Spider plant

CHLOROPHYTUM COMOSUM

Don't let the name keep you from growing this easy-to-grow, low-light-loving plant. It is known for reducing indoor air pollution. Keep it in well-draining soil and out of direct sunlight for best results. Repot in spring if roots start growing outside of the drainage holes.

Why we love it: Spider plants come in green or variegated varieties, and often form new plantlets at the end of their long, arching stems.

‹ Prayer plant

MARANTA LEUCONEURA

A prayer plant's leaves close vertically in the evening, resembling praying hands, hence its common name. Avoid using hard water because this plant has a sensitivity to fluoride. Another watering tip: Use water that is room temperature for best results.

Why we love it: It is extremely tolerant of low-light conditions and actually prefers indirect sunlight.

PRAYER PLANT: DEAGOSTINI/GETTY IMAGES

^ Lucky bamboo

DRACAENA SANDERIANA

Known for its straight stalks and lush green foliage, lucky bamboo needs low, indirect light to thrive. Try it in an office or a bathroom. Be sure the roots are covered in water, changing the water every two to four weeks. Transplant into soil with good drainage, and water often—but be careful to avoid waterlogging.
Why we love it: While it's not the same as the bamboo used for feng shui, it still reduces stress.

^ Peace lily

SPATHIPHYLLUM SPP.

A common mistake when growing peace lilies is under- or overwatering. Check the soil with your finger before watering to see if the plant is actually in need of a drink. Repot once peace lilies outgrow their pots. Skip growing peace lilies if you have pets or small children.
Why we love it: Peace lilies are favorites because of the dark green leaves and white flowers. For more blooms, expose the plant to more light.

› Golden pothos

EPIPREMNUM AUREUM

Golden pothos, also known as devil's ivy, is an ideal low-light houseplant because it purifies air and actually grows best in indirect light. Beware: It's poisonous—definitely skip this one if you have young children, cats or dogs, and wear gloves when handling the plant to avoid a possible rash.
Why we love it: It's incredibly hardy, growing in dry soil or in a vase filled with water.

LUCKY BAMBOO: ALUXUM/GETTY IMAGES; PEACE LILY, GOLDEN POTHOS: DEAGOSTINI/GETTY IMAGES (2);

^ Snake plant

SANSEVIERIA SPP.

Almost impossible to kill, snake plant is easily recognized by its long leaves with yellow or silvery white stripes. You may also know this hardy houseplant as mother-in-law's tongue.

Why we love it: It does well with moderate watering. Allow the soil to dry completely, checking it once every two weeks.

^ Monstera

MONSTERA SPP.

Also known as the Swiss cheese plant, monstera is recognized by its large split leaves. Repot it once a year while it's young to freshen soil and encourage growth.

Why we love it: For a houseplant, it grows surprisingly fast, so it will quickly add life to an office space or a large room. In its natural habitat, this tropical jungle plant reaches 10 feet tall or more.

‹ Chinese evergreen

AGLAONEMA SPP.

All a Chinese evergreen needs to thrive is regular watering—but avoid cold temperatures and excessive sunlight. Allow the top of the soil to dry slightly between waterings. If you have sensitive skin, wear gloves when handling it.

Why we love it: This common plant is available in 22 varieties and is known for bringing good luck. Consider giving it as a housewarming present.

What Are Your Best Houseplant Growing Tips?

Readers share trusted tricks for success with gardening indoors

When my inside potted plants are dry, I put ice cubes on top of the soil to slowly melt and water the plant without flooding the pot. It's easy, there's no mess and I'm less likely to overwater this way.

Lisa Sherman CARLSBAD, CA

Collect rainwater and use it on your houseplants. I've been doing it for years!

Sharon Woodworth GEORGETOWN, KY

Always check with a moisture meter before watering.

Louise McVay WALESKA, GA

Move houseplants outside in summer. They love rain, heat and humidity. Bring them in before the first frost and spray any insects with an organic insecticide to prevent the bugs from moving into your home.

Lynn Jones SALEM, IN

I water houseplants with water I've boiled eggs in. It works better for me than any commercial plant food!

Sandy Lewis AKRON, OH

I read that sprinkling the dirt with cinnamon prevents powdery mildew, so I gave it a shot—it worked! I no longer have a problem with the disease.

Jeanine Buettner KALISPELL, MT

BLOOMSCAPE (2)

Indoor Harvest

Grow garden-fresh ingredients year-round

By Niki Jabbour

G**O AHEAD AND** keep on gardening even after autumn weather arrives. Many edibles, such as tomatoes and strawberries, can be grown indoors all winter long. Follow these simple steps for creating a robust indoor garden.

Light Is Essential

"If you are going to invest time, effort and money into indoor growing, quality supplemental lighting should be your No. 1 priority," says Leslie Halleck, the author of *Gardening Under Lights: The Complete Guide for Indoor Growers*. "Tomatoes and peppers need the equivalent of full sun conditions indoors, for a long enough duration, to provide meaningful harvests."

Leslie uses ceramic metal halide high-intensity discharge 315-watt grow lamps to fruit her tomato and pepper plants indoors. She says you can also use a large T5 fixture (which holds eight lamps) with high-output T5 fluorescent lamps. For some dwarf cherry tomato varieties, you can use smaller LED fixtures and a bright window.

Pamper Plants with a Grow Tent

Serious indoor growers may want to consider a grow tent. These handy setups grant more control. "Grow tents create a microenvironment where you can manage light, temperature, humidity and photoperiod," the number of hours of light that a plant needs in a day, Leslie says. Some grow tents can accommodate tomatoes and peppers, as well as cucumbers, beans and squash.

Pollinate by Hand

Flowers of indoor fruiting plants need to be pollinated to develop. Wind-pollinated plants like tomatoes can be given a gentle shake from time to time to spread their pollen to other blooms. For crops like strawberries that are normally insect-pollinated, use a paintbrush to move pollen from the male stamens to the female pistils.

Edibles to Grow Indoors

Tomatoes

"They typically produce well with about 14 to 16 hours of light," Leslie Halleck says. Tomatoes thrive in temperatures between 70 and 78 degrees. If space is an issue, grow compact dwarf varieties like Lizzano, Tiny Tim or Micro Tom, all of which are ideal for pots.

Peppers

Put peppers, particularly hot peppers, in planters to grow indoors. Give them 14 to 16 hours of light, and temperatures around 70 to 80 degrees. Plant spicy habanero, jalapeno or Red Ember, or try sweet Cupid peppers.

Grow peppers in a pot with good drainage.

Lemons

Look for a spot in your house that offers lemons bright light and cooler temperatures. "Lemons bloom year-round, so you can have different stages of ripeness at the same time," says Steven Biggs, author of *Grow Lemons Where You Think You Can't*. "Plus, they have a fantastic fragrance when they bloom." Start with a Meyer lemon—a kitchen staple that Steven says is prolific and relatively low maintenance.

Strawberries

The compact size of strawberry plants makes them a good choice for indoor growing. Leslie suggests looking for a day-neutral variety, as these are typically the easiest to grow indoors. Plant them in 6-inch pots, adding a bit of compost to the potting mix to enrich the soil.

More Edibles for Indoors

Try cucumbers, citrus, salad greens and herbs.

LARS CHRISTENSEN/SHUTTERSTOCK

Make Your Poinsettias Last

Keep spirits bright with this classic plant, even after the holidays are over

By Helen Newling Lawson

Many cultivars feature beautiful multicolored bracts.

CLOCKWISE FROM LEFT: JULIE GARRARD/GETTY IMAGES; SUNTORY FLOWERS; BASIEB/GETTY IMAGES; BREEDER: LAZZERI GIOVANI PIANTE, SUPPLIER: SYNGENTA FLOWERS

Princettia Indian Red

A LITTLE GREENERY IS the perfect antidote for post-holiday blues. Here is how you can keep your poinsettias pretty nearly all year round.

Start with a healthy, fresh plant. Houseplant grower Costa Farms says if the tiny flowers in the center of the colorful bracts are green buds, not brown or producing pollen, the plants will tend to keep their color a little longer.

At home, keep the plant away from drafts and heat, which include doorways, vents and fireplaces, and in a very sunny spot—the pros at Costa Farms emphasize that "poinsettias thrive on sunlight."

Poinsettias also need water, but not too much. Jim Faust, an associate professor of plant and environmental sciences at Clemson University, says, "Watering once per week is sufficient," depending on the size of your plant and the conditions in your home. "Overwatering tends to be more of a problem than underwatering," he says. And it can cause the plant to lose leaves early.

Watering too often can also lead to root rot. "Never let the pot sit in water," Jim says. Be sure to remove the decorative foil wrapper, which can trap water.

Despite your best efforts, your poinsettia will likely drop most of its leaves by March or April. Once that happens, cut it back to 6 to 8 inches tall. Keep it watered and in a sunny location. You can even take it outside for a summer vacation.

With filtered sunlight, ample water and feedings of liquid fertilizer, your poinsettia should be an easy-care patio plant. Be sure to bring it back inside before the risk of frost, check it for pests and treat it if needed.

Getting a poinsettia to regain its festive color is a little trickier. This requires some hard work and dedication.

Starting in October, give your poinsettia about 14 hours of total, continuous darkness in a space that's a little bit cooler than 70 degrees, followed by 10 hours of bright light. A dark closet and a grow light on a timer work well. Just remember to keep it watered. You can also cover the plant with a box each night and put it in bright sunlight each morning. With a little luck and perseverance, your poinsettia will be as beautiful as when you first bought it.

Alaska

Poinsettias Galore

More varieties to fit any occasion.

Multicolored: The bright pink and white bracts of Christmas Beauty Marble make a splash. Superba New Glitter dazzles with red leaves and splashes of sparkling white.

Compact: Princettia is a very popular smaller poinsettia, grows in an attractive shape and is available in a few colors.

All White: Alaska is one of the brightest white varieties and also has holly-shaped leaves.

Not Just for Christmas: Autumn Leaves add some orange flair to Halloween or Thanksgiving. Use a pink selection like Bravo Pink for a fun Valentine's Day centerpiece.